The loose women Book for Lovely Mums

Also By

loose
women

Girls' Night In
Here Come the Girls
The Little Book of Loose Women
Loose Women On Men

The loose women Book for Lovely Mums

HODDER &
STOUGHTON

First published in Great Britain in 2011 by Hodder & Stoughton
An Hachette UK company

1

Loose Women is an ITV Studios Ltd Production
Copyright © ITV Studios Ltd 2011
Licensed by ITV Global Entertainment Ltd
Illustrations © Marjorie Dumortier

A CIP catalogue record for this title is available from the British Library.

ISBN 978 1 444 72867 5

Typeset in Adobe Caslon by Hewer Text UK Ltd, Edinburgh
Printed and bound by Clays Ltd, St Ives plc

Hodder & Stoughton policy is to use papers that are natural, renewable and recyclable
products and made from wood grown in sustainable forests. The logging and manufacturing
processes are expected to conform to the environmental regulations of the country of origin.

Hodder & Stoughton Ltd
338 Euston Road
London NW1 3BH

www.hodder.co.uk

Contents

Introduction   1

Pregnancy and Babies   4

Our Mums   34

Motherhood   71

Kids   102

Sex   146

Dads and Relationships   161

Mums and Work   186

Mums Were Kids Once, Too   204

Acknowledgements   227

By day she's Meryl from Accounts, but
by night she's...SUPERMUM!

Introduction

Put your feet up, ladies, because you're in for a treat. This book is for lovely mums everywhere and that includes you. Yes, you! Who else dishes out her love by the bucket-load? Who else provides a constant flow of solace, cuddles and advice? Who else can banish nightmares with the touch of her hand? And let's face it, when it comes to juggling time, balancing plates and pulling stuff out of a hat at a moment's notice, no one else even comes close.

It makes you wonder where the world would be without mums. Weirdly empty, for starters, because there would be no human race. No mother love, no mother comfort, no mother tongue, no mother's ruin! There's a very strong chance there wouldn't be any sticky toffee pudding, either. Life simply wouldn't be worth living!

Since ancient times, the cult of motherhood has been

celebrated across the globe. Classical paintings and sculptures in every culture depict saintly mums cradling, sheltering and protecting their young. You don't see many iconic images of them dashing to do the school run, putting in a full day's work, tripping over the vacuum cleaner, burning the tea, arguing with teenagers, taking elderly parents shopping, soothing hubby's ego or keeling over with exhaustion, but there you go. Life was a lot simpler back then, apparently.

This, then, is our testament to mums and motherhood, where we share the highs and lows of being a parent, from the moment of conception to the day the kids fly the nest – and way, way beyond. Here's where we remember our own mums' efforts (legends, all of them!), cringe at childhood memories, hold forth on how to keep the kids in line, discuss the lot of the working mum, try to include dads in the whole parenting debate (sigh!) and think back to when we first learnt about the birds and the bees. What, you thought we wouldn't be talking about sex, for once? Do us a favour! This book covers *all* things relating to maternal matters, no holds barred!

It's full of the strong opinions you've come to expect from

your favourite loose ladies, along with all the wit, wisdom and wackiness that tends to go along with them. Here are Coleen, Denise, Sherrie, Carol, Lynda, Jane, Lisa, Zoë, Andrea and Kate at their sharpest best, at their gooey, softest worst, and everything in between! Some of us may not be mums, but that doesn't mean we don't have forceful views on matriarchy! Take it from us; this is the complete motherlode.

It's not always easy being a mum. But it can be a lot of fun. Either way, we wouldn't swap it for the world. (Apart from those of us who don't actually have kids, or want them, thank you very much!) And we love our own mums beyond belief, even when they're driving us insane with their eccentricities. Actually, especially then! Those of us whose mothers are no longer with us still really, really miss them. After all, no one can replace your mum. There's simply no one like her. Can you think of anyone else who would have gazed into your squidged-up, wonky face on the day you were born and thought they were seeing an angel?

So this book is dedicated to wonderful mums everywhere, with the utmost respect and admiration. Along with a dash of cheek, a splash of sauce and a whoops, I burnt the sausages!

3

Pregnancy and Babies

It all starts so well, doesn't it? What could be better than a roll in the hay, a playful romp between the sheets? Next comes the wonderful news that you're expecting a baby! Nothing could be more exciting; everything is going swimmingly. But suddenly you find yourself feeling sick, tired and grumpy, and people keep mistaking you for Willy the Whale. Grrr! Then the contractions come, you're wondering what hit you, and bang! – you're weeping with joy and love over your very own weeny Winston Churchill. So do you deserve special treatment through this weird and wonderful time? And is it the be-all and end-all? What's best, boy or girl – or would you just be better off getting a dog?

* * *

The fun part

I always wanted ten kids, but then I realised what you had
to do to get them and I thought, actually, no! *Coleen*

I've never looked at a bloke I've gone out with and
thought: I love you so much, I want to have your
babies. But I've often looked at a bloke and thought, I want
us to do what you do to try and have babies! *Carol*

I didn't plan Matthew. I simply became pregnant
early on in my marriage to Tim. After he was
born, I wasn't very well, so we weren't going to
have any more. Then, aged about ninety-seven,
Louis was another wonderful suprise! *Denise*

* * *

She may have got her picture in the paper, but being an Octomum wasn't all it cracked up to be!

A whale of a time

When I was pregnant, I decided that I was the only pregnant woman in the world. I felt that special. I thought, no one can do this like I can. This was in the early stages. In the latter stages, with Ciara, I was brought back for a scan at five months because they said it must be twins – and it wasn't. People would come up and say, 'Not long now!' and I'd say, 'Another four months, actually.' All I was missing was a trunk when I was pregnant! *Coleen*

I was enormous when I was pregnant. Doing the weather at *GMTV* I blocked most of Ireland and, indeed, parts of Cornwall! *Andrea*

It took me a long time to have Keeley. So when I finally got pregnant, I went out and bought a kaftan at five weeks! 'What *have* you got on?' people asked, especially as I didn't show until I was about seven months. Then, when I got to seven and a half months, I put on four stone just like that. I could have filled two kaftans! All I ate was mashed potato and gravy. It was so bad that, after I'd had Keeley, I had nightmares about all this mashed potato running down the street trying to swallow me! So don't ever get a craving when you're pregnant, girls, because it will come and get you!   *Sherrie*

★ ★ ★

Pregnancy scares

I had Beau at thirty-five and even then I don't think I was mature enough. I wasn't even mature enough to check the test you pee on to find out if you're pregnant. I was so scared that I got Paul to go and check it, so he knew I was pregnant before I did!   *Lisa*

While I was pregnant, I did a show at Wembley Arena. On the day of the show, I had a car accident, which really shook me up. Afterwards I thought, I can't feel the baby kicking, and I got a bit worried. The choreographer said, 'Right, we're going to get the doctor in.' So I had a DIY scan in the dressingroom wearing a pair of sparkly shoes.

The runner came up and said, 'Four minutes until you go on stage!' They put jelly on my belly and gave me a scan. I heard a heartbeat and burst into tears, because I was so happy. Then I high-fived the runner, legged it onto stage and said, 'Good evening, Wembley!' Suddenly all was good in the world.   *Kate*

* * *

Raging hormones

You can't control your hormones when you're pregnant, so it can be hard to get a grip on your emotions. You're feeling things you've never felt before; sometimes they're nice and sometimes they're not. I was quite stressed, aggressive and angry when I was expecting, partly because I was the size of a house at four months, but also because I just felt tired and grumpy. I remember asking to go for a wee in a shop once.

'No, sorry,' the woman said nastily.

'Hello?' I said, pointing to my pregnant belly. 'I really need to go.'

'No, it's staff only,' she said.
'Scuse me!' I shouted, and then we had
this big argument that I would never
normally have got involved in!   *Zoë*

I haven't had a baby, but I do understand the hormone thing, obviously. As any woman who's ever had PMT knows, even though you're kind of aware of what's going on, you can't control it, which makes you even angrier. I accept that, but I do sometimes think that pregnant women think that they can behave in an exceptional way, just because they're pregnant. I know a lot of women who behave as though they're the first woman in the whole wide world to get pregnant and have a baby. That's fair enough, because it is a miracle happening and it might be the first time they've ever done it, but they seem to want special treatment, which isn't fair. *Carol*

Would you give your seat up for a pregnant woman? *Zoë*

No, because you're not ill, you're pregnant! Excuse me, you're not an OAP, you're not disabled; you're just pregnant. Hang on, I pay for my seat too! *Carol*

It's not a pretty thought, but I would like to sneak into Carol's bedroom in the middle of the night with a turkey baster and make her pregnant! I really, really would! *Denise*

Yeurch!!!! *Carol*

★ ★ ★

The really difficult bit

For the majority of women, childbirth is painful. If you don't believe it, get hold of your bottom lip and try stretching it over your head!   *Coleen*

I'm sure childbirth is not a nice thing to go through. But what I don't understand is, once you've been through it, why do you have to go on about it all the time? Sherrie's daughter Keeley was born twenty-five years ago and Sherrie's still going on about how painful the birth was!   *Carol*

I had the most wonderful pregnancy. I was very big – I put on four stone – but it didn't worry me. I was as happy as the day is long. My problem came when I went to have Keeley, because I got to the hospital and these funny pains came. I thought, what's that? I had more contractions and I cried out, 'Oh my God, what's this? I'm not having this pain! I'm not having this baby!' The hormones make you insane. So at twelve o'clock, I put my coat on and got my bag and started to leave. Luckily, a nurse came running after me and took me up in the lift to the birthing room, where they lay me down and gave me pethidine. So everything was fine and happy in the end!   *Sherrie*

When my mum was in labour, she went on the bus to the hospital, because my dad was at work. In those days, men didn't come in for the birth. My dad just got a phone call to say, 'There's another one! Clear the drawer out.' I really was stuck in a drawer; how bad was that? Not that bad, I suppose, as long as they didn't shut it. Maybe that's what happened to me – lack of oxygen! I said, 'I hope I was top drawer, not bottom drawer, Mother!'   *Coleen*

I have a feeling that many men don't want to watch their partner giving birth. 'You must, if you love me!' the woman says. But if they don't really want to and afterwards they have this image in their heads that they can't dispel, it may make love-making that much more difficult for them.

Either way, this is the time that things start to go wrong in the bedroom in a lot of marriages. That period when the children are young, and the mother is focused totally on them, is bloody hard. It should be discussed more, so that it can be sorted out. *Lynda*

When I gave birth, I felt like a Supermum. I felt like I was the only woman who had ever given birth. I wanted a podium, the National Anthem and a medal. *Coleen*

★ ★ ★

Baby love

I don't think anyone can explain the fear that you feel from the moment your baby is born and they hand it to you. It's terrifying when you go home for the first time and you're left on your own. Shane Junior was a nightmare to get to sleep and when he finally started sleeping, I'd be so relieved. But then I'd start listening for his breaths and worrying. Is he breathing? I'd take the blankets off to check and he'd start crying again! And I'd think, oh God! Here we go again!   *Coleen*

When Keeley was born, they put her face next to mine. I heard the midwife say, 'Now that's true love.' And it's been true love ever since.   *Sherrie*

Those first moments as you're leaving the hospital with your baby in her carrycot are very strange. You've got a baby there and you don't quite know how it got there! You think someone's going to come up to you and say, 'What are you doing with that baby?' *Lisa*

Babies make a horrible noise. They're angry, because they don't want to come out of that cosy, comfy little place. As soon as they get out, they're like, 'PUT ME BACK IN!' *Carol*

★ ★ ★

Cutie pies

I don't think all babies are cute, especially not when they've just come out. It takes time to grow into your face. I'm still waiting! But I am polite when proud parents show me pictures of their baby and say, 'Isn't he lovely?' 'Yeah!' I say, because they're full of happiness and I don't want to ruin the moment by saying, 'Actually, he looks like Charlie Drake!' *Lisa*

You know the saying: 'Every cockroach
looks lovely to its mother!'   *Lynda*

People always think their own babies are cute and I think
you're obliged to go, 'Aaaw, isn't it lovely?' even when
you don't know what 'it' is. So I do, I say, 'Aaaw!' Then
I say, 'Right, can I stop now?' and walk off!   *Carol*

Don't forget that some people are beautiful when they're
little and horrible when they grow up!   *Lynda*

My niece won't mind me saying this, but she was very
ugly when she was a baby! My sister sent me a photograph of her and I honestly couldn't stop laughing. (She
grew up to be a gorgeous girl – she's fifteen now.)
I was working as a producer on *The Big Breakfast* at
the time. I thought, this is a really good idea! Let's
get people to send in pictures of their ugly babies, or
ugly photos of themselves as babies. We could not
believe the response. We had thousands. We used

to open up sacks of baby pictures in the production office and laugh all day long. People loved it. We put all the pictures up on a big board, the viewers voted for their favourites and the ten winners came in, as grown-ups. Honestly, it went down a storm! *Carol*

Sometimes little babies are quirky looking and that's what makes them so adorable. I love it when they have little orang-utan bits of hair sticking out on top of their heads! *Andrea*

★ ★ ★

Assisted conception

Having kids by IVF is quite a good idea. You miss out the middleman and still get the kids! *Coleen*

I think IVF is a massive business that preys on vulnerable, desperate women. *Carol*

'Look, my Tarquin is going to be the next Picasso!'

As much as I slag off my children, bless 'em, I always wanted kids when I was growing up. If I couldn't have had them, I would have gone through anything, so I think it's a miracle that doctors can give couples IVF treatment.   *Coleen*

I've never had that absolute longing for a baby, but I know many people who have. To take the hope of having a baby away from them would be heartless, so I think IVF should always be available on the NHS.   *Jane*

* * *

Superannuated mums

A dear friend of mine has been trying for a baby for over ten years, by every route possible, and is now, at fifty-one, having her first baby via egg donation. This woman is a powerhouse, a dynamo.

She and her husband are loving and committed;
I think they're going to be the most incredible parents. Their baby is due any week now.

I was thinking about my friend when I was doing
my big shop yesterday. There was a woman in her
twenties in front of me who had obviously just
had a baby, but you could see that she was a lady
of size even before the baby came along. She was
so unhealthy that even unloading her shopping
onto the conveyor belt was making her breath-
less. I thought, hang on a minute. Who's a fitter
candidate for motherhood? My friend at fifty-
one or this young lady whose trolley showed
me exactly why she is the way she is? *Kate*

The way we're going with plastic surgery, we'll have
a woman of seventy-five with a wind-tunnel face
rocking a baby saying, 'Isn't it lovely?' *Lynda*

I had a phone call the other night. It was my sister saying, 'You have to phone Maureen!' I had about ten missed calls and I was thinking, please don't tell me you're pregnant, Maureen. You're fifty-six! I'd be so embarrassed. Anyway, she wasn't. She'd just won on the bingo! *Coleen*

★ ★ ★

A right or a wrong?

Obviously, it's very sad if a woman is desperate for a baby and there's no one to have one with. But I don't know how we got to the stage whereby it seems OK for a woman to create a human life by any means whatsoever, like using a male friend's sperm. Maybe it's because I don't understand what it feels like, but I find it all a little bit disturbing. There are other ways you can look after children, if that's what you want to do, but I don't agree with the idea that it's your right as a woman to have a baby. It's not a right; it's a gift – a miracle. You're really lucky if you can do it. But now women plan it. 'I'm not going to do it this year; I'm going to do it next year. I'm going to wait until I'm forty; I'm going to have IVF.' I'm not saying people shouldn't do it, but if I'm asked, I'll say that I think there's something wrong with it.   *Carol*

I understand the desperate need to have a baby, but we all have desperate needs and it doesn't mean that we can fulfil them. I have a desperate need to win the lottery every Saturday, but it ain't gonna happen! So if you desperately want to love someone and you can't have a baby, for whatever reason, either adopt, or buy a puppy!   *Coleen*

* * *

Babies having babies

Should we have antenatal classes for teenage mums at school? No! How far are we going to go? Crèches in school for the pupils' kids? We should go the other way and show teenagers the hardship involved in having a child, not make it easier for them.   *Coleen*

When they're thirteen or fourteen, get them to look after a little baby for a day and have it scream in their ear for hours. That'll put them off!   *Zoë*

Maybe we can teach girls that there are other options than getting pregnant. You don't have to get pregnant to start a new life, to find love, give love or be loved. You can do it another way.   *Sherrie*

I think children should all wear chastity belts until they're twenty-five!   *Jane*

What would be really shocking is if people were prosecuted for having underage sex! *Lynda*

* * *

An ideal age

In defence of younger women, I've a mate who had a child on her own when she was sixteen and she has always been a phenomenal parent. Her son is a really well-balanced child. She had the right personality and maturity at sixteen, whereas I was thirty-five when I had Beau and I was one of those 'helicopter' parents that they talk about, flapping over the kid, saying, 'Do you want this? Can I get you something? Oh no, she's breathing funny! She's looking funny!' I wasn't calm and capable, even though I was a much older parent, so I think it depends on the individual as much as their age. *Lisa*

* * *

Baby substitutes

It took me eight years to have Keeley and in the meantime I had an enormous Weimaraner dog, who became my substitute for a baby. Then, when Keeley was born and I had a real baby, my other baby, my dog, looked after her. He used to stand and look at her for hours. He loved her so much!   *Sherrie*

I have several friends who don't have children and without a shadow of a doubt their dogs have become child substitutes. I feel that child substitutes are always the worst-behaved dogs. When they take a chunk out of some little child's face, the owners will say indulgently, 'He's only playing! He likes you! It's just a little nip.'

They don't discipline their dogs. They have a tendency, in the words of one dog trainer, 'to Disney up' their dogs. It means they don't tell them off or school them;

they let them sleep in the bed with them! It's no good for the dog, because dogs are pack animals.   *Denise*

I'm not a big child lover and I'm not a big animal lover. But I *do* like white carpets! That's why I don't have anything around that makes a mess.   *Jane*

★ ★ ★

Boy or girl?

When I was pregnant, I was convinced I was having a boy. Then I had the scan and found out it was a little girl. I was worried, because I thought I might be hard on a daughter. I'm quite direct, the type that says things like, 'Pull yourself together!' So I thought I wouldn't be sensitive and girly enough to bring up a daughter.

In actual fact, it didn't make a blind bit of difference. I was thrilled to bits that I'd had a baby girl

There had been a girlfriend once, yes, but no one had quite lived up to his lovely Mum.

and she's just wonderful and easy to look after and reason with. It's totally different having boys, it seems. I see my mates with sons and the way they talk to them: 'Sit!' 'Put it down!' 'Get over there!'   *Lisa*

I was very nervous when I was pregnant with my first child and found out he was a boy, because I knew nothing about boys. We were all girls in my family. What would I do with his willy? The minute you change that nappy, you are literally faced with the fact that your child is not a girl!

As it turned out, I loved having boys. There is a special relationship between mothers and sons, because you're different sexes. Your little boys are so affectionate to you when they're young! One son used to play with my hair every time he had a drink. It was wonderful. The terrible thing is that it stops. You wake up one day, when they're about twelve, and it stops.   *Lynda*

★ ★ ★

Transformation

What's the old saying? 'Men get married hoping that women won't change, and they do. Women get married hoping that men will change, and they don't.' I personally know people who have married someone that maybe they weren't completely in love with because they wanted children. And after they've had the children, it's like he doesn't exist. I feel so sorry for men in that situation.   *Carol*

When you have children, your priorities change and you become much less selfish. You become self-less, actually. You tend to forget about yourself and concentrate on the kids and your husband. All of a sudden, two years down the line, you say, 'I really must go out shopping for myself one day.'   *Coleen*

★ ★ ★

Mums first!

Instead of having a 'Baby on Board' sticker, I sometimes think I'll get a sticker that says, 'Suitcase in the Back'. All right, so you've got a baby. Big deal! Loads of people have babies. Don't worry; I'm not going to crash into you. I'm a safe driver.

Why do mothers and babies have car parking spaces right by the door? Why do they have to be right by the door? They can be over on the other side of the car park: what's the difference? Women with children are not disabled; they just have children and that's their choice! It's not my problem.   *Carol*

The other day, I parked in the mother and child bay at the supermarket, with my mother in the car. A man came up and said, 'Sorry, you can't park there.' I said, 'Excuse me, I'm the child and she's my mother!'   *Jane*

I hate prams as much as people with no kids do. I hated them before I had kids and I still hate them now that Jake is eight. When people run into your ankles, you want to kill them! *Zoë*

What is it about mums with new babies? Why do they suddenly think they have right of way everywhere they go? You know, when you're walking down the road and there's a mum pushing a pushchair; there's not much space in the road and they walk in a straight line, expecting you to get out of the way. What is that?

I think we over-accommodate people with children, and children themselves, especially in restaurants and bars, where frankly they shouldn't really be!!! I was once told off for using a mobile phone in a restaurant. I wasn't talking loudly, but I was told I wasn't allowed to use a phone, so I said sorry and put it away. Across from me, there was this kid going, 'Aarrggghhh!' at the top of its voice! Where's the sense in that? *Carol*

I get pram rage sometimes, because people don't get out of my way! It's actually far more difficult to change direction when you've got a pram than it is for someone sauntering along to side-step and walk by.   *Andrea*

I don't complain about children. All I complain about is children making a horrible noise in restaurants, and buggies everywhere. You can't get round the supermarket because there are so many of them! All pushchairs should be left outside the shop.

I have slight baby phobia, to the point where my friends don't even bother to tell me when they've had their babies anymore. It's not that I'm not interested, but I'm just not interested!   *Carol*

Our Mums

According to psychologists, your relationship with your mum is the most important relationship of all. It influences everything from your ability to form bonds to your attitude to sex. It also fills you with love, wonder, anguish and all manner of sensible sayings, while driving you up the bloomin' wall every now and then! Yes, the ties between mother and child can be exceedingly complex and a little bit crazy. But we wouldn't have it any other way, would we?

My mother was the powerhouse of the family
and I grew up thinking that women rule. I don't
think I've ever stopped believing that women run
everything, while at the same time making men
believe that they have all the power. *Sherrie*

My mother has never let me down, in any shape or form. She's my best friend, my confidante, and I would always turn to her in a crisis.   *Jane*

Everybody says it and it's true: you don't really appreciate your mum until you have kids.   *Andrea*

We have few such special relationships in our lives: grandmas, mothers, fathers, granddads, children. You have to cherish them and put the work in to get the best out of them.   *Kate*

* * *

Maternal advice

My mother always used to say, 'Make the best of yourself,' and I've always tried to follow her advice. So I won't even go out to the dustbins unless I'm in full make-up!   *Sherrie*

'Mother and daughter? Surely not!
I presumed you were sisters…!'

My mum didn't give me any advice, really. She was very conscious of letting us do what we wanted and letting us learn from our mistakes. The only time she ever recommended something to me was when I first started going out with Chris Evans and she said, 'He's lovely. You should marry him.' And I did! But my mum wasn't a very good judge of compatibility when it came to men, unfortunately.   *Carol*

Whatever happened in my life – when people hurt me, or when my first love let me down – my mum would say, 'Don't worry. What goes around comes around.' In actual fact, she was right. But there was one thing she always said to me that I couldn't bear: 'There's plenty more fish in the sea.' I swear that if I ever say it to my boys or Ciara when they're upset, I'll hit myself. When you're heartbroken, you think: I don't want just any fish! I want *that* fish!   *Coleen*

My mother used to hate it went I went on holiday, because she didn't trust aeroplanes. She never

flew; she never left the country, not once. She was a total home bird. Every time I used to get on a plane, she'd say, 'Don't do it. I don't trust it. Don't go!'

'Why?' I'd ask.

'Because if man was meant to fly, he would have been born with wings.'

'Don't worry, Mum,' I'd say. 'Millions of planes take off every day and they don't crash.' But it never, ever made her feel any better.   *Carol*

My mother did a lot of character building with me. I remember falling in love with a boy who looked like Paul McCartney when I was around thirteen. All we ever did was hold hands; I don't think he even kissed me. I had a fixation on Paul McCartney then – and still do. I've always fallen in love with anyone who looks like him.

One day this boy told me that he didn't want to see me anymore. I absolutely wanted to die. Back at home, I went in to see my mother, who was in bed with some kind of flu. 'I'm very sorry,' she said, when I told her what had happened. Then her tone became stern. 'Right, stop now. It's gone. Over. Time to move on.' This jolted me out of my misery. 'OK,' I whimpered. I went out of the room and cried a bit more, but her approach helped me get over it quite quickly and has helped me in everything I've subsequently been through. After a cry at home, I'll say to myself, 'Right, that's enough of that. Get on with the rest of your life.'   *Sherrie*

* * *

Viewers' views

We asked viewers to email in their mums' words of wisdom for our Mother's Day feature, 'Mum's the Word'. Here's a lovely one from Janey in Berkshire:

'A saying that's been around for decades in our family is, "If everyone threw their troubles in the air, you'd be glad to catch your own." It's a good way of putting things in perspective.' *Andrea*

From Anne: 'Years ago, my sister's boyfriend of three years was a singer and a guitarist. My mother told her that she was wasting her time with him, as musicians never earn any money. The ex-boyfriend is now one of the richest men in the UK – Paul McCartney!' *Zoë*

This one's from Linda in Barnsley. She says, 'When my mum was entertaining, she would always say, "Keep them laughing. They won't eat as much."' Good advice! *Carol*

* * *

A girl's guide

My mother guides me in a very quiet way. She never does it about business, because that's where my strength lies, but she's guided me in my personal life a few times – or tried to! In life, your mother's voice is always there – especially mine, as she lived in the next room for years!   *Jane*

My mother said, 'You have to learn to be a secretary.' Well, I went into the office once. Then I went back the next day and the man had died! It's not right, is it?   *Sherrie*

I was always musical and then I went into singing. My parents said, 'As much as we think you're going to make it, get a back-up plan in case you don't.' So I learnt shorthand, typing and commerce. I have to thank them for that, because now I do all my own secretarial work, so I've saved a fortune!   *Jane*

My mum never told me not to do anything, because I think she sensed that if you tell a kid not to do something, they'll want to do it even more. But it didn't stop me rebelling and trying to find things out for myself. For instance, I started smoking at a ridiculously young age. I don't smoke now, but back in the early 1970s I was determined to be a smoker. My first fag made me feel so sick, but I persevered. I was desperate to get into it, because everyone else was doing it! *Carol*

When my marriage ended, I wrote a song for my mum called 'The Hand that Leads Me'. It's about how she took my hand, like she did when I was six, and said, 'We'll get through this together.' She led me through the darkest time of my life and I'll always be grateful that I had her around. Sometimes she didn't even have to say anything: she just put her hand out and touched my knee and that was enough comfort. *Jane*

When you're young, you don't listen to your mother, do you? It doesn't matter what she says. My mother said to me so many times, 'He's wrong, he's wrong for you.' I went exactly the other way, because that's what you do. Yet you know what? She was right. I can say that now, with hindsight. But you can't be guided by somebody; you have to learn for yourself. You've got to make your own mistakes, come a cropper, pick yourself up and then go back and say, 'Mum, you were right. I'll listen to you from now on.' *Sherrie*

I didn't realise quite how much my mother's influence guided my life until I stepped back a little bit. (I used to live with my mother, I don't know if you know!) She was always 99% correct, so I'm glad I had her influence, but it got to the point where the line between us was blurred. Without my parents' guidance, I could well have gone off the rails, but now I'm thirty-one – don't laugh! – I think I maybe should start growing up. I've been very dependent on my mother and I did everything for my mother's approval. I still do, in fact. If she's not happy with something, it'll definitely give me second thoughts. *Jane*

Subconsciously you pick up and pass on your parents' lessons about life and morality. I now give my kids advice that my mum used to give me all the time.   *Coleen*

My mum, God rest her soul, truly believed that if you gave people enough love, it would be returned. That's not always the case, but it's a good way to live.   *Lynda*

Mostly, my mum let us make our own mistakes, which I think is a really good way to learn. I chose not to go to grammar school, even though I passed my eleven-plus. She didn't say to me, 'You're going to the grammar school!' She said, 'What school do you want to go to?'   *Carol*

My mum has an amazing quiet strength. I've learnt from her that you don't have to raise your voice to be heard. Sometimes the quieter you become the louder the effect is. She has also taught me that stillness can be a really strong quality. It's come in very handy at work.

I hosted an event up in Scotland a few years ago. It was a big do; there were 700 people. Everyone was throwing the drink back and having a fabulous time, but they were getting quite rowdy and I wasn't sure what to do about it. So I did nothing. I just stood back from the lectern, went quiet and looked at them the way my mum used to look at me for carrying on. Everyone went, 'Oops, sorry!' They were all as good as gold after that. *Andrea*

* * *

Being open

I'm very open with my children. I don't sit them down and tell them everything I've done in the past, but if they come to me with any problems or ask me a question, I always answer as honestly as possible. I think it's because when I was younger, my parents didn't answer any questions. My mum's answer to everything was, 'Don't worry, you'll find out soon enough.' My children also know where the line is. I don't want to just be their best friend, because I'm their parent as well. They can come to me with anything, but they can't always expect me to say, 'That's OK, son.' Sometimes they'll get the lecture from hell.   *Coleen*

My mother is my best friend. I can tell her anything and she has confided in me too. I know an awful lot about her and she knows absolutely everything about me. It's a trust we've got. She's the one person I can go to and say, 'I don't know how I'm going to handle this.' If she's been through it, she'll say, 'Well, I did it this way.' Or, 'Don't do it that way, because I did that.'   *Jane*

* * *

On partners

You can't slag your partner off to your mum, because your mum remembers everything. Even when everything is lovely again and you've forgotten about what came before, your mum remembers!   *Andrea*

My mum always tried to tell me what she thought of my ex. She predicted that it would all end in tears. But you know what? If your mother says something like that, you go the opposite way. It taught me a lesson: don't interfere. Just listen and be support-ive. So now, even when I want to say something to Keeley, I think to myself: shut up, Sherrie! Hold it back. It's none of your business.   *Sherrie*

People often say that if their parents tell them to do one thing, they automatically want to do the opposite, but I've never been like that. Even now, if my parents say, 'Oh no, we're not sure . . .' I'll go along with what they advise.   *Andrea*

* * *

The fashion gap

My mum was a very smart dresser. She liked a blouse and wore nice trousers, or slacks, or whatever you want to call them. She was a big fan of the designer Jacques Vert. I never borrowed any of her clothes and I know that she used to look at what I used to wear and think, stop it! Yet she always told me I looked nice.   *Carol*

Have you ever seen the film, *The Sound of Music*? Where she makes the dresses out of a set of curtains? Well, we really were the von Trapp family. We matched the cushions on the couch! If you came to our house, people would plump us up to sit on!   *Coleen*

Would I ever wear something to match my daughter's outfit? Hmmm . . . Amy's favourite outfit is a little fairy dress, with wings on the back, and wellies, so I'm seriously thinking of getting a set myself.   *Andrea*

Even though the girls were in their thirties,
Deborah still insisted on the Von Trapp look.

I had no choice about what I wore as a child. We had hand-me-downs; that was it. Whatever we could get our hands on, we wore. It was always itchy jumpers that felt like sand-paper on your skin and looked like they'd been boiled! But we wore them anyway. We didn't want to freeze! *Carol*

There was a disco for under-sixteens called Zone 22 behind the ice rink at Whitley Bay, where I spent many a happy hour, let me tell you! Once, my mother made me wear a shirt and a cravat, and I already had ridiculous hair. I remember a boy coming up to me and saying, 'Are you a lad or a lass?' *Denise*

When you're eight or nine, you start to find a style. I always wanted to wear jeans, which I wore with bumper boots. I had really short hair, so I looked like a tomboy, but I used to get really upset with people saying to me, 'Alright, sonny?' So I wrote in to a comic – I think it was *Bunty* – and said, 'I'm really upset because everyone thinks I'm a boy.' All they said was, 'Grow your hair and wear a dress!' That was it. I thought: thanks very much, very helpful! *Carol*

My mum, bless her, always dressed really well. But everything she wore was second-hand. She just couldn't bring herself to spend £50 on a dress. 'But I can get it at Margaret's for £2.50,' she'd say. She'd get a cheap pair of shoes and dye them to match the dress, and then make her own matching handbag. She was brilliant, actually. But when you're a young kid or a teenager, you really don't want to wear homemade gear, do you?   *Coleen*

I know that my mum totally disapproved of me dressing up in a bin-bag and fishnet stockings, with a safety pin in my mouth, and going up to London, watching punk bands and gobbing on people. I was only a weekend punk, but she disagreed with it. She would never, ever have said so, though, because she knew that everything she disapproved of, I would just enjoy doing more.   *Carol*

If I had come downstairs dressed in a binbag with a safety pin in my mouth, my parents would have dropped down dead!   *Andrea*

My mum used to buy me some very strange things, normally from second-hand shops. I had some shocking flowery dresses when flowery dresses weren't in anymore. She'd say, 'It looks fine on you,' and I'd be thinking, 'No, it looks hideous.' *Coleen*

My mum used to make most of our clothes! I protested at loads of things, but as my mum laughingly recalls, 'You were always the one that we could talk round.' I remember I took part in a public speaking competition and my mum said, 'Why don't you wear that jumper that Granny knitted you? She'll be so proud.' Well, my mum used to perm my hair and I had acne at the time, so there's a photograph of me in the local paper looking absolutely hideous, with a home perm and spots, wearing a mint-green jumper with brown flowers on it! I look at it now and think, no wonder I had no boyfriends! *Andrea*

★ ★ ★

Are you ever too old for a cuddle?

We're a very tactile family and I am particularly cuddly and kissy with my daughter Keeley and grandson Oliver. I never stop kissing Ollie. He won't like it when he's thirty-five, will he?   *Sherrie*

My family were always slightly reserved about cuddling, but my mother is a great cuddler. She wouldn't come up and cuddle me all the time, but if I do go up to her and say, 'Can I have a hug?' she always gives me one.   *Jane*

My mum gave me lots of hugs, but she wasn't overly cuddly. I remember her saying to me as a grown-up, 'Just because I don't show it doesn't mean I don't feel it.' I respect that.   *Andrea*

★ ★ ★

The seal of approval

I still seek my parents' approval, even now. It's hideous. I pretend that it doesn't matter if they're not in favour of something. I say, 'I'm just going to do it anyway!' But inside I'm thinking, I really wish they'd approve. Just because it's easier.   *Andrea*

The really annoying thing is that my parents are mostly right!   *Andrea*

It's the same with my mum! I hate that, don't you?   *Jane*

I think you should both grow up!   *Carol*

★ ★ ★

That special relationship

It's a fallacy that you shouldn't get on with your mother-in-law. Having said that, I didn't have mothers-in-law with my first two husbands, because they were both dead. But I get on perfectly well with my third husband's mother! *Lynda*

Ray says to me that if his mum hadn't liked me, that would have been it. He wouldn't have gone with me. I'm gutted now. I should have been more horrible to her! Actually, we get on great, but if she had hated me, things would have been different. Ray idolises his mum. He spends a lot of time with her, goes home to Blackpool every week, takes her shopping and does loads for her. She's on her own now and so she always comes to us for Christmas and things like that. If she hated me, it definitely would be a problem for him – and for me, because I'd probably hate her back! *Coleen*

I'm not the perfect daughter-in-law, but I get on well with Mark's mum – and it's not just because we're nearly the same age! It's a bonus, but I don't know if it would be that important if we didn't get on well.   *Carol*

I think Ronaldo's mum would quite like me. What have I got to offer? Well, he looks a bit too perfect, doesn't he? He needs a bit of a rough up. And I'm the girl to do it!   *Coleen*

There are a lot of mums out there who prize their sons and feel that there isn't a girl in the world who's good enough for their little soldier.   *Carol*

★ ★ ★

Keeping in contact

My fiancé Mark is certainly not a mummy's boy, but he calls his mum a lot and I like that. I think it's really lovely. It makes me wish that I'd called my mum every single day when she was alive. She's not there now, so I can't call her, and I think, make the most of it, because you really, really miss your mum when she goes.   *Carol*

I used to ring my mum every single day, but we didn't really have anything to say to each other. It got to the point where the pauses started becoming like little rows, little niggles, because you end up aggravating each other. Paul phones his mum once a week and he does it religiously and has a really good long conversation about Beau and how we all are, as well as checking that she's alright. Unless someone really needs looking after, I think once a week is enough.   *Lisa*

Girls ring their mums to talk about secret things and physical things: what she should do and how she should do it; all those kinds of things. My daughter and I text each other ten times a day!   *Sherrie*

Every night when I go to bed, I say a little silent prayer: thank you very much for my healthy baby

and please make sure he phones me when he's older.
It is a genuine fear of mine that he won't! *Kate*

★ ★ ★

Like mother, like daughter

I aspire to be like my mother because I admire her in so many ways, so I actually don't mind turning into her. I welcome it, really. She's always been very nurturing and I want to be like her. But it's so funny, because when it comes to my relationship with Ed, she'll say things like, 'Don't be doing that for him! Start as you mean to go on.' And yet she would be the first to do it for my father. So I'm saying, 'Hang on a minute! Double standards here?' But thank you, Mother, for doing my ironing. I love you for that! *Jane*

As time's gone on, I have become exactly the same as my mum. I don't know if that's because we all start caring about the same things when we get to a certain age, but

Although their view of the nuptials was slightly
obscured by the Mother of the Bride's enormous
hat, they all agreed that it was a lovely wedding.

I said to Beau the other day, 'You're not coming out with me wearing that!' The times my mum used to do that to me and I'd think, I would never do what she did. But I think it's inevitable and I'm kind of glad it is. I like the way the generations follow each other in that way. *Lisa*

I've turned into my mum! I hear myself saying things like 'Have you eaten?' *Jane*

I went completely the opposite way to my mum. I remember her standing at the kitchen sink almost her whole life, peeling potatoes. Drudgery it was, just drudgery. She was a single mum with four kids, but not through choice, and she had to deal with it. I registered this and thought, I'm not going down that road! So I scooted off in the opposite direction and I'm the total opposite of my mum. She never travelled; I travel all the time. She had four kids; I don't want kids. There are so many things I've done differently. *Carol*

* * *

Your mother's genes

I flinch every time I do something and think, ooh, my mum did that! I don't know why, but I don't like it. When I first started seeing Mark, I bought a butter dish. I got it home and thought, oh my God, that's just like my mother! She always had a butter dish. But I can't have a young boyfriend and a butter dish, because he really will think I'm an old granny! *Carol*

The one thing I think I inherited from my mum was her metabolism. In other words, the fat gene! My mum was always a big lady, but my dad never went above 9 stone, even though he ate like a horse. I just really hated him for that! Why couldn't I have inherited that gene? *Coleen*

What characteristics have I inherited from my mother? Well, my mum liked a drink now and again, and I definitely inherited that from her! *Carol*

My kids get any nasty traits they have from their fathers. Every time they do something bad, I say, 'Oh, they're just like their father.' When they do something really lovely, I say, 'They get that from me!'   *Coleen*

* * *

Mystery mum

I knew little things about my mum and I knew her as a person, but I didn't know that much about her. I think it's a generational thing. The people from her generation were much more private. Now, people are obsessed with telling everybody everything about themselves. We do it every day on *Loose Women*. People get on Facebook and MySpace and Twitter and tell everybody about what they're doing. But perhaps it might be nice if people were a bit more private and kept stuff to themselves . . .   *Carol*

My mum and I get on very, very well; we're a really close family. But she's my mum. She's not my best mate or anything like that. There's lots that I don't know about her. She still surprises me even now that I'm a proper grown-up, because she's sharing more with me as I'm getting older. As kids, we're always shocked to think that our parents had a life before we came along.   *Andrea*

Some parents tell their kids everything because they want to offload stuff. I've got friends who do it. But I never really knew that much about my mum and her past, although towards the end of her life she started to tell me things. In a way, I felt a little bit guilty that I didn't know about these things before, maybe because I'd never asked. When I thought about it afterwards, I thought, I wish I hadn't known, because some of the things were pretty awful. Still, she didn't repeat the behaviour, which I thought was quite admirable. That's being a good parent. She just allowed us to be children and didn't burden us kids with the stuff that went on in her early life. I thought that was pretty good.   *Carol*

★ ★ ★

At home

My mum was a farmer's wife. She worked hard all day, and I mean hard labour, but at four or half four you'd walk into a warm room where there was toast and jam and a cup of tea. Why would you want to go out then, after that? I truly think that if young men could come home to that it would stop a lot of trouble.

Nurturing has gone out the window a bit, because everybody's chasing the dream and everybody's gone out to work. I know it's necessary, but to me one of the single biggest factors in the breakdown of teenage society is not having anybody to come home to. The classic thing with teenage children is that they don't want to talk to you, but if you're not there, they miss you!   *Lynda*

A sense of belonging is so important. I used to love the feeling of coming home to Mum and Dad when I was young.   *Coleen*

* * *

Leaving home

My mum was glad to get rid of us, to be honest! I'm not saying that's a bad thing; I think it's quite right. She'd done her bit and she'd never been happier than when she lived in a one-bedroom bungalow, because that meant we couldn't keep moving back home. That's a fact! I did see a lot of her, but it was really important to her for us to be independent. She wanted us to go and do our own thing and live our own lives.   *Carol*

* * *

My mum, the hero

My mum was my hero when I was sick. Nobody holds your head or rubs your back better than your mother when you're blowing your groceries, let's be honest! She was always there with a Jaffa orange and a *Bunty*.   *Coleen*

My mum was always my hero when I had to get up at four in the morning for work and she brought me a cup of tea!   *Jane*

I remember my mum being quite brave when a load of mods and rockers turned up to my sister's twenty-first birthday. The rockers had arrived on bikes with heavy chains and inevitably there was an incident; it looked like there was going to be a big fight outside. My mum and dad were farmers and Mum had put a poorly little lamb in the bottom of the Aga, with the door open, to keep it warm. She went outside just as the fight was about to kick off and said, 'Hello, would you like to see a little lamb?'

'Yeah, OK,' the rockers grunted, and they went into the kitchen, where Mum gave them all a cup of tea. 'Oh, it's really sad. Is it going to be alright?' they kept saying. They spent all night in the kitchen with my mum and the lamb! *Lynda*

There are so many things that your parents do for you. Mine were my heroes every day. When we were touring, my mum used to fly over to Japan with a suitcase of tea bags and real butter! That was a hero moment for me. I'm not sure I would go that far for my children. *Coleen*

* * *

There's no telling her

My mother is in her late seventies now and she will insist on carrying four bags of shopping on the bus, which means that she has to walk all the way to and from the bus stop with them too. I say to her, 'Look, next to the bus stop there's a taxi rank. Why don't you just get a taxi?'

'Mum, I'm 37 and clearly capable of
cleaning behind my own ears!'

'I've got a bus pass,' she says. 'I don't need to get a taxi.'

I think, what's the matter with you? You can afford it. Don't spend so much on the shopping and then you'll have enough left for your taxi! But no, she likes her bus, mainly because she likes to tell every-body on the bus what we're all doing. *Jane*

* * *

Losing your mum

My mum died in 2003 and everything switched off. Something inside you dies when you lose some-one you love – for a while, at least. My mum was the most important person in the world to me. She had such a massive influence on my life. She was the first person I really knew and loved who died. I was probably quite lucky to get to forty-three without knowing anybody who had died. Luckily, time does heal. You learn to live with it. It took me about three years to wake up again.   *Carol*

Looking at pictures is the way I remember people, along with the memories that I have in my heart, which will always be with me. I've got a lovely picture in my bedroom of my mum with Ciara.   *Coleen*

★ ★ ★

The life and soul

I don't get a chance to throw a party very often, so when I do it's a proper party and it goes on for hours! There's usually a band, the neighbours are all invited and my mother's still up at four in the morning doing vodka shots, long after I've gone to bed. Most of the time she doesn't really drink. But at a party she can down them and not even flinch, and so can I. We're made of good, strong stuff.   *Jane*

Motherhood

What exactly defines motherhood? Is it a physical fact, a state of mind or a way of being? Does cooking have to play a part? Or can you get away with doling out toast and vitamin pills? Perhaps it's all about keeping house and creating a warm, loving environment. Or can you leave all that to their dad? Maybe the key is to appear really, really grown-up. Get lost! Whatever happens, we'll still ignore the bills, embarrass our kids and stop at nothing to win the mum's race at sports day!

* * *

The greatest love of all

I love being a mum. It came home to me last weekend when Ciara was vomiting in a bucket while I was picking fleas out of her hair. *Ah, motherhood!* I thought.   *Coleen*

My greatest joy is being with my daughter and my grandson. If I don't see them for a week, my brain turns into scrambled egg and it kills my heart, because seeing them is what I live for. People accuse me of living my life through Keeley and Oliver. But I don't live my life through them: I live my life with them and for them.   *Sherrie*

We all want to be heroes to our children, but we fail every day. You're just about to crack it, you're just about to save the kitten from the tree, and the ladder breaks!   *Lynda*

* * *

The domestic goddess

I am so far away from the idea of the domestic goddess!
I feel guilty that I can't cook, because I have tried.
Famously, I have a photo of the sausages that started
out as a sausage casserole and ended up burnt to a char.
I actually had to throw the saucepan away! The problem
is that the phone will ring or something more interest-
ing will happen and I get distracted. Also, when I do
present any food to my children, who are twenty-one and
nine, I put it down in front of them and they exchange
a look that says, 'Ah, bless!' Luckily, their dad is a great
cook. And Matthew is roughly the same age as Carol's
boyfriend, so obviously he can fend for himself!   *Denise*

Paul always gets into the kitchen first. His father
was a chef, so he's a really good cook. When I come
home from work, he's already at the cooker. (It's not
like I walk really slowly from the car to the house or
anything!) When he's away, Beau will say, 'Oh no, not

vitamin pills again, Mum!' because I'm such a bad cook that I use them as a meal replacement! *Lisa*

I'm Miss Old-Fashioned. I like looking after my man and being in the kitchen, in my pinny – nothing else, just my pinny! I like cooking and nurturing. But you know what? My next-door neighbour said to me, 'If you think for one minute that nurturing, cooking and cleaning up after a man is going to keep him, you're wrong.' And maybe she's right! *Zoë*

My idea of making a meal is reading the back of a packet to see how long before the microwave goes ding! I just physically haven't the time to be peeling potatoes and have pans boiling up everywhere. It would be lovely if I had all day, but I haven't! *Jane*

Like my mother, if I haven't cooked enough, I'll go without. I would never say to my husband or one of my sons, 'I haven't done enough, so you're not having any roast potatoes, because I'm having them.' Having said that, it's only about twice a year that I do cook! I'm definitely not a whizz in the kitchen.   *Coleen*

You know what Jerry Hall said about being a chef in the kitchen, a maid around the house and something else in the bedroom? I'll take the third one, thanks!   *Carol*

I used to do it all: the cooking, the cleaning, the washing, the ironing, and it's all a load of old trollocks!   *Sherrie*

I love cooking and I love creating a homely environment. When people say that women shouldn't take on these stereotypical roles, I don't quite understand it, because I get such pleasure from seeing people sit round my table, or come home to a cup of tea and a piece of toast.   *Lynda*

The other day, Louis was looking forward to sausage and mash, which I did my best to cook. I cut the sausages in half before I fried them and they curled up in the frying pan. 'Mummy,' Louis said, distraught, 'you've made me mashed potato with burnt curly worms!'   *Denise*

My mum's a bit like Mrs Doubtfire, the typical old-fashioned mum really. She can cook, she can bake and she makes everything from scratch. I'm very lucky really. Her cooking is second to none and I love her shepherd's pie.   *Jane*

I can't cook and I don't want to learn because then I'd have to do it!   *Denise*

It seems that scientists, or 'researchers', have found the perfect excuse for men to get out of doing the housework. A study – conducted by a man, I might add – has found that household chores, including using a vacuum cleaner or a microwave oven, could reduce a man's chance of having children by lowering his sperm count. Yeah right, and I'm Dolly Parton!   *Kate*

★ ★ ★

Food, glorious food

When I lived with my mum, the only thing we ever argued about was her food shopping addiction. Every single cupboard was chocka, the fridge was chocka, the freezer was chocka. 'We're not in the war anymore!' I'd say.

'But our Tony likes these cakes,' she replied.

'But, Mum Tony doesn't live here. I do!'

At my mum's, there's a four-course meal at three o'clock in the morning if you want one. At Sunday lunch, the joint would be enormous, just for the two of us. 'Who's coming?' I'd ask.

'We'll use it up tomorrow,' she'd say. But we never did! Old habits die hard. She still cooks for a family of five. *Jane*

I associate the family with cooking. So even when there's nobody there, I cook for a hundred people, just in case somebody pops by! I would die if my son turned up with a friend and there wasn't enough food for them. *Lynda*

My mother said to me the other day, 'I'm not going to lie to you. You're putting a bit of beef back on. But you've got a long day ahead, so here's a bacon sandwich.' You can't win! *Jane*

Kids are terrible about eating the same things twice. I put a piece of beef in a sandwich for my son and he says, 'Uh, I had that yesterday!' I say, 'No you didn't! You had it *hot* yesterday. Now you're having it *cold*.' *Lynda*

★ ★ ★

Before and after

When I had Keeley, we didn't really take into consideration that we had a baby and tried to carry on with our normal lives. I liked to play darts and I remember thinking that patting baby and throwing a double top didn't work somehow, because I wanted to use the same hand to do both. You had to remember to throw the dart and not the baby!   *Sherrie*

I'm a very responsible parent, but I also like to party. When you have children of course your life's going to change, and your kids become your number one priority, but what gets me is the drastic transformation in people. We have friends who used to come round on a Friday, have a few drinks and maybe just crash upstairs. Now they have a child, they say, 'Can't stay, because Baby Jimmy has to be in bed by six-thirty.'

'But it's a Friday night,' I say. 'Why don't you just put Jimmy to bed upstairs and have another glass of wine?'

Kate only realised something was wrong when
she tried to breastfeed the orange juice.

'Oh no, because we have to get Jimmy into his own bed at the same time every evening . . .' Yawn-o-rama!

'Shut up!' *Denise*

I think you do grow a little bit boring when you become a parent. So what? Yes, I am a little bit boring, but I'm a mum, and Jake's more important than me getting trashed every weekend! *Zoë*

* * *

That elusive maternal instinct

I've never really been maternal, but I do have a maternal streak. In other words, I'm quite motherly, just not with children! As they say, I do love kids, but I couldn't eat a whole one. *Jane*

Having a child may have crossed my mind once, for about five minutes. But then I started thinking about it and I decided, no! I'm way too sensible for that. It's too easy to say, 'What if you'd met Mark ten years ago?' Well, he would have been seventeen, so it would have been no good! Even if he had been older, I don't think it would have changed anything. Now I think I'm too old to have a baby. The moment's gone, if it was ever there, but as far as I'm concerned it wasn't.   *Carol*

I think people are either maternal or they're not. Take Carol, for instance – it ain't happening, is it?   *Zoë*

I have spent a lot of my time justifying my decision not to have children, usually to people with children. I find their attitude a little bit offensive and rude, because I would never go up to a woman with children and say, 'Oh no, why did you have them?' Yet they come up to me all the time and say, 'You've not got any children? What a shame!' What gives them the right to say that? It's almost as though women with children are acting as though they're in the right and they're treating women without children like weirdos. It's just insane.   *Carol*

I've spoken to a lot of women who have said, 'I never wanted to have children. I don't have to have them. Why did you have children?' I feel like they're almost having a go at me for having them!   *Coleen*

People think that because you're a woman and biologically made to have children, you should have them. I've never really had that urge to have children and I'm really glad that I didn't, because I would still have to be in touch with the partners that I've had in the past. God forbid!   *Jane*

I think of myself as child-free and not childless. Not having children has become more of a life-style choice for some women.   *Carol*

* * *

Role reversal

A couple of years ago, I came in after a bit of a party night and my son Matthew said, 'Do you know something? It's more like having a teenage daughter than a mother!' Then he said, 'My life is like one continuous episode of *Absolutely Fabulous*!'   *Denise*

Sometimes your kids turn into mini-parents. One night after the euphoria of *Dancing on Ice*, we were back at the hotel celebrating. It got to about half past twelve and Ciara, who was sitting opposite me, said, 'Mum, I think it's time for you to go to bed. You've got work tomorrow.' 'You're right,' I said. As I went into the bedroom, I thought, wait a minute, my seven-year-old daughter has just sent me to bed!   *Coleen*

I was going out on a Saturday night wearing a little bit of a blingy dress, which was just above my knee. 'OK, darling,' I said to Louis, my youngest, 'we're staying at a hotel tonight. Mummy loves you and I'll see you tomorrow.'

He held up his hands. 'No,' he said, shaking his head, sucking in a breath and wincing. 'Too old for that dress!'

There was another time when I was feeling really premenstrual and having a horrible time. I was getting ready, feeling fat and my make-up wouldn't go on. 'Mummy, you know the Bride of Frankenstein?' said Louis.

'Yes,' I said.

'She wants her head back.' Horrible!   *Denise*

I treat my mother like a five-year-old sometimes. She'll be cooking and I'll say, 'Ooh, put a bit of seasoning in.'

'What's going on?' she says. 'I've been cooking your meals for forty-odd years and now you tell me I'm doing it wrong.' *Jane*

When I was ill one Christmas night, Jake, who was sixteen at the time, stayed downstairs with me, because I was in a lot of pain. I kept saying to him, 'Jake, just go to bed, I'm fine.'

He turned round and said, 'Mum, how many nights have you sat with me?' Ah! How sweet!

I said, 'You're right. You've got the rest of your life to pay me back!' *Coleen*

Sometimes I revert to being a child when I'm with my parents, especially when it's anything to do with money. I'll say, 'Daddy, somebody sent me a really horrible brown envelope with a window in it and I want you to deal with it.' Also, my dad still cuts my bacon sandwiches into quarters! *Denise*

I taught my boys how to shave their faces. They just watched me doing it first!   *Coleen*

* * *

Good sports

When Shane was five, he joined a weekend football team and he played all the way through his childhood. He absolutely loved me going to watch. It was a big part of my life and I miss it now. It was fantastic being there, cheering him on.   *Coleen*

I must admit that I was quite happy when Finlay stopped playing football. I liked it when he took up karate and swimming, because it was inside!   *Andrea*

I always went to cheer Keeley on. I used to want to be in the netball court with her, shooting at the net, because I was so excited! 'Come on, girls!' I'd shout. I felt like it was me and Keeley against the world and she had to win! At one match, I kept saying to the woman standing next to me, 'Have you seen that girl playing with Keeley? She's useless, absolutely useless. She can't play netball!' Of course, it turned out to be the girl's mother and she never forgave me.   *Sherrie*

In my experience, if you're freezing by the side of a football pitch on a Sunday morning, you're not going to be very vocal, because it's too blimmin' cold to shout! Having said that, when I go and watch Jake kicking a ball around every week, his little face lights up when he sees me coming. Our kids definitely need our praise and encouragement.   *Zoë*

* * *

Competitive mums

Something odd happened to me at Beau's sports day last year. Most of the mums don't go in the mums' race because they say it's a bit of a bun fight. There are even some mums who take it quite seriously and put their spikes on! *Oh, those competitive mothers, what are they like?* I thought. It's just a bit of fun!

Well, Beau said, 'You're going in the mums' race.'

'OK,' I said. I was really nervous and psyched up, because I felt like I had to win, for Beau, because she was new at the school.

Also, people kept saying, 'Are you going in the mums' race? You're really brave, aren't you?' I was so charged up!

When I got to the starting line, the headmistress came over and gave us each a balloon to put between our legs, to make it more fun. I thought, where's the fun in that? Now we're ridiculous and we can't really have a race. In fact, what was more ridiculous was how much I wanted to win the race for my daughter.

So we all started with the balloons between our legs, hobbling along for a bit. Then some people's balloons popped and they started to run. I saw one mum whip the balloon out from between her legs and start running with the balloon in her hand. I thought, *right, game on!* and took my balloon out. I was like Forrest Gump: 'Run, Forrest, run!' I was so nervous and charged up but I won it!

I felt rubbish afterwards. *Lisa, what on earth happened to you?* I thought. Haven't you grown out of that horrible, competitive, must-win-and-be-first mentality? Aren't you a much more sedate, serene person these days? Well no! Obviously not. *Lisa*

* * *

'No one gets away with hurting my
little Sammy Sausage...'

Meddling mums

If my daughter got married, I would never interfere. I would have nothing to do with the wedding whatsoever. The only things I would be interested in are where it was, what she was wearing, the bridesmaids, the pageboy suits, the groom, the balloons, the flowers and the invitations. But nothing else! *Sherrie*

There's a difference between being a meddling mum and being a caring mum. Meddling is when every boy or girl they bring home is not good enough and you're constantly giving your opinion or advice when it's not asked for. My mum never meddled in my relationships. She didn't get involved in making decisions for me; she never said, 'I don't like him,' or anything like that. Even when my mum and dad thought that maybe I wasn't making the right decision, they just waited for it to fall apart and then they were there for me.

It's funny now, having kids of my own. I try not to be an interfering mum, because I really don't want to be like that. But I've noticed that if Shane or Jake has a girlfriend and I say, 'She's lovely. Her laugh drives me nuts, though,' then three days later they finish with her. 'Why?' I ask, and they say, 'Well, you didn't like her laugh.' I'm frightened to say anything now! So when they ask, 'Did you like her?' I reply, 'Yes, yes, she's lovely!' You feel really responsible.   *Coleen*

Certainly, I've been a little scary with Keeley's boyfriends and I think I did frighten a few away. But I thought it was the right thing to do, chasing them down the road shouting, 'Go! Go!'   *Sherrie*

I don't think I'm a meddling mum. I try very hard not to involve myself at all in my children's lives, but two of them live with me, so it's hard not to be involved!   *Lynda*

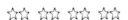

93

I don't meddle in my children's lives. I do phone them a lot, but it's usually to say, 'Are you passing the offie? Can you bring me some wine?' Only joking. No, I phone Matthew a lot, but that's because I love him and he drives a car ... *Denise*

Den, you've gone through his phone and taken all his friends' numbers, so you'll always know where he is! *Coleen*

That's because I pay for his phone, so when it's never answered, it does my head in! He never answers his phone. So when it's lying around, I think, I'll just get this number and that number, so I've always got someone to ring to see if he's alright. *Denise*

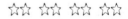

I've taught my boys to cook and I would love
them to leave home. I suggest it frequently!
But where are they going to go?   *Lynda*

★ ★ ★

Only children

Jake begs me all the time for a brother or a sister. He
goes to my friend's house and she has three kids. The
little one, who is three, says, 'Jake, will you put my clips
in?' and he does what she asks and looks after her.

He says, 'Mummy, Mummy, I want a baby sister!'

I keep saying to him, 'Darling, it ain't going to
happen!' I need a boyfriend first! I don't want another
baby, anyway, because Jake weighed ten pounds
when he was born! Ideally, I want a boyfriend with
kids, so that Jake can have a brother and sister

that way. I'm not having any more ten pound-
ers, thank you very much! I've done my bit.   *Zoë*

I still feel guilty about not having had another child and
given Keeley a brother or sister. But I justify it to her by
saying, 'I would have had to share you with another child
– and I had you all to myself, which was what I wanted.'
Thankfully, although I think she's missed out, she doesn't.
'Get over it, Mum,' she says. She's quite happy.   *Sherrie*

I've got my little Jake, my beautiful Jake, who I love more
than life itself. I think that if I had another baby, how would
I possibly spread my love? I have friends who've had second
children and they say, 'The first one is getting in the way!'
or they shout at them because they've put their foot in it.
I think it's so hard and I don't know how I'd do it.   *Zoë*

★ ★ ★

The guilt factor

Women have always striven for perfection. We live
on guilt. It's always guilt, guilt, guilt! *Sherrie*

I don't think women necessarily strive for perfection. It's just that, with many things, if we don't
do it, it won't get done. Men don't suffer from
the guilt thing in the same way. *Denise*

I grew up with my mother saying, 'Girl, you've more money
than sense!' That has stayed with me, which means that
I hesitate about paying someone sixty or seventy pounds
to massage me for an hour, but I would spend the same
amount on my children or my husband at the drop of a
hat. I'm just in that maternal phase in my life where you
treat everyone else and don't really treat yourself. *Coleen*

I'm sick of living with guilt. I go to bed with
guilt, I wake up with guilt . . . *Denise*

Who is he? Can I have a bit? *Sherrie*

Apparently, if the mother is the one who smokes in a family, it's much more likely that the kids will end up smoking. That makes me feel very guilty! My kids don't smoke, as far as I know, but who can be sure? I hope not, because Ciara's only eight! It's hard to lecture them about it, but at the same time I'm the parent and I'm old enough to say, 'If I could go back, I would never have had that first cigarette. Once you do that, you're hooked.' *Coleen*

★ ★ ★

To-do lists

Every night, I write down what I've got to get done the next day. *Kate*

You know what? I couldn't even be bothered looking for a pen to do that. *Coleen*

I have to write it down because I don't remember!   *Kate*

You don't remember? You need to go
to the doctor, then.   *Coleen*

But surely you can't remember everything you need to do in a day?   *Denise*

If I can't remember it, then it wasn't important.   *Coleen*

Good point.   *Kate*

But sometimes I can't remember who
I am, admittedly!   *Coleen*

* * *

The fear factor

I'm so scared of everything now when it comes to my kids. When Ciara plays out in the back garden, I'm watching her constantly, thinking, *someone might be able to get over the fence!* I really fight against getting so paranoid that I'm wrapping her up in cotton wool, because where is it going to end? You let your kids go back to their friends' houses for tea. What's the next step? 'Well, I need to do a police check on you before she can come back for chicken nuggets and chips.' It's all getting out of control.   *Coleen*

For parents, the fear is, in most cases, greater than the reality of the threat. I think people are over paranoid and too scared; sometimes it's completely out of proportion. But what can you do?

I'm more fearful now for my sons, who are older, than I am for Ciara, because Ciara's still in my control. I know where she is, who she's with and what she's doing. The boys are now out in the big bad world on their own.

'See you later, Mum, I'm just going out,' Shane says.

I say, 'OK, I love you,' and I give him a hug. When he gets to the car, I run out and say, 'I love you!' and hug him again.

'You've just done that in the kitchen,' he'll say.

'I know, but it might be the last time.' (Sob!)

'But I'm only going to the garage!' *Coleen*

Kids

It's the question on every mum's lips: is there a right way to bring up children? Anything can trigger the doubt: the wild screaming insanity of a toddler's tantrum; the relentless cheek of a demanding ten-year-old; or a solid wall of surly teenage silence. What's a mother to do? Grapple with the unanswerable or run screaming for the hills? The best advice seems to be to follow your maternal instincts and draw on your astounding resources of love. Failing that, where's that bottle of wine?

You do anything for your kids, because you love them.
It's just something that's in you, naturally.   *Kate*

It's hard to choose the kind of parent you're going
to be. We're winging it half the time, anyway.

We don't know what we're doing! *Lisa*

I'm really glad I don't have kids, because when they get to eighteen, they clear off and they don't even say thanks! *Carol*

I can't understand these people who have eighteen children and then say, 'I'm still broody.' That's got to be some kind of mental illness going on. I mean, I can't cope with two, with a blooming nanny and my husband at home half the time! *Denise*

* * *

Praise matters

I know it sounds ridiculous, but when you have a naughty child of two or three and upwards, you are supposed to praise them when they're good at every opportunity. I've seen it work. When they're naughty, yes, you chastise them and punish them, but when there's a glimmer of goodness, you praise them. It's called positive parenting and it's exhausting, but it works! If you emphasise the good behaviour, they tend to realise that if they're good, they're going to get something nice, and then the bad behaviour eventually diminishes. *Zoë*

I went horse riding in Cornwall a couple of years ago and met a lovely girl who had left her job in a nursery because the political correctness had just gone too far. She had been told that she couldn't say to little Simon, 'Ooh, Simon's got some new shoes! You look handsome in those shoes!' because that would breed an arrogance in him in later life. I just think that's the world gone mad! *Denise*

★ ★ ★

To spoil or not to spoil?

When Ciara was six, she asked me if she could have a mobile phone, because a lot of her friends had one. 'Yes, of course, darling,' I said, 'when you're about twenty!' *Coleen*

I spoilt my daughter, but she's grown up to be very nice, because I also taught her how to be a good, kind person who respected her mother and grandparents. *Sherrie*

The first thing my kids asked me when we bought our new house was, 'Is there a pool?' I said, 'No, you can have a rubber paddling pool like everybody else!' *Coleen*

It's important to try and counter materialism with spiritualism. Tell them, 'It won't actually make you happy to have that computer before anybody else. It doesn't ultimately make you happy to have eighty-five pairs of trainers. Be your own person.' *Lynda*

I think this generation of children is totally spoilt, and not just in a material way. Children have been given too much power; they have too many rights and they're aware of them all. Parents now are scared to discipline their own children, in case they get disciplined by the state. So you end up with a lot of unruly kids who have no respect for authority, no respect for their parents, no respect for anybody, not even themselves. They know all about their rights but they have no sense of personal responsibility and I think that's really dangerous. There's a whole generation that's going to take years to fix, if anyone knows how to fix it. I don't. *Carol*

People have always accused me of spoiling Keeley. But you know what? She's turned out to be the most beautiful human being, so I must have done something right. I don't think I've spoilt her. I've just loved her beyond the point of duty. Loving someone a lot can't be wrong, and it's the same with my grandson Oliver. *Sherrie*

There were times when I hovered over Beau, because I didn't want to get it wrong. It's a really important, responsible job that you're doing, so you can get a bit obsessed with it. I don't think it's a great way to be, but I can understand why some people get like that.   *Lisa*

There are boys that are mummy's boys and you want to slap them, don't you?   *Sherrie*

* * *

Performing monkeys

I don't like it when parents overindulge their children. You'll be sitting having dinner, or coffee, with grown-ups, and a child will come in and start showing off. Suddenly all the adults will turn to the child and say, 'Oh look! Aw!' while I'm carrying on, talking to myself! If I were the parent, I'd say something like, 'We're having a conversation. Go away and come back later.'   *Carol*

I didn't want to perform as a child. I was the one behind my mother's skirt. I loved music, but I was painfully shy. It used to make me feel sick if someone asked me to sing. I couldn't do it and my mum and dad never forced me, for which I was very grateful. Then, later in life, all of a sudden I was fine.   *Jane*

Louis has a good sense of humour and I'm always saying to him, 'Tell everyone that joke!' or 'Do your karate!' But he won't do it on demand. He chooses his moment, thank you very much!   *Denise*

★ ★ ★

'Pushy Mum, moi?...Well, someone needs
to pay for the extension!'

Scary monsters

Kids love getting scared. We've got to stop wrapping them in cotton wool. You've got to prepare them for the world: scare 'em stupid! Children definitely know the difference between fantasy and reality. When I was younger, and this was a very long time ago, there was a film called *Them*. It was all about giant ants and it used to scare us to death, even though the special effects were rubbish. But we couldn't get enough of it! *Carol*

Do you remember when *The Texas Chainsaw Massacre* came out? One day I went to my friend's house and her big brother had some friends round who brought the video with them. I knew I wasn't allowed to watch it, but I did. Because I was the youngest, I knew that they'd take the mickey out of me if I screamed, so I sat at the back and stared at a tiny corner of the screen for the whole film. Oh my goodness! What a horrible film. I had nightmares for weeks and I couldn't tell my mum and dad why! *Andrea*

I recently went out and bought some new books for Ben, including some of the titles I remembered from child-hood, like *Hansel and Gretel* and *There was an Old Lady Who Swallowed a Fly*. I got them home and started reading them and they're horrific! For a start: 'There was an old lady who swallowed a fly. I don't know why she swallowed a fly. Perhaps she'll die.' She goes on to eat a load of animals before carking it. Then there's Hansel and Gretel: two poor lost souls, abandoned by their parents, go walking in the woods and get taken in by an evil witch who tries to boil them and kill them. Night night! Sleep well! *Kate*

Kids love anything horrific. The more revolting, the better! Real life is much more scary anyway, so I think you're just getting them ready for it. *Lisa*

I love seeing kids scared. There's nothing better than being at a fairground and seeing children coming off the ghost train in tears! *Carol*

My daughter Beau loves stories, so for her last birthday we found a professional storyteller who knows two thousand stories. She rang me up and said, 'What sort of things do you think the kids would like?' 'Fairies and dragons, that sort of thing,' I said. I told Beau, 'I've organised a storyteller. You've got fairy and dragon stories.'

'No, no!' she said. 'We want really scary stories, with people getting their heads cut off and things like that!' Kids absolutely want to be horrified.   *Lisa*

* * *

Bedtime reading

In my experience of talking to other mums and dads, it seems that no matter how well read or encouraging the parent is or isn't, your children will decide for themselves whether they're into books or not.   *Denise*

I used to record audio CDs for children profession-
ally and proudly play them to my children. We'd all
start listening and within seconds I'd be fast asleep
and snoring. I'd bored myself to sleep! *Lynda*

Louis loves being read to, but he won't let me
do the voices, which I get really fed up about.
'Mum, can you just do it without the voices?' he
says. Try saying that to an actress! *Denise*

My boys don't read at all, even though I read to them
all through their childhood and they loved it and read
for themselves. At some point I lost them – I don't
know whether it was because of football or computers – and I feel very guilty about that. *Lynda*

Matthew wasn't interested in reading when he
was younger, but he loves all kinds of books
now, including philosophy books! So you can
never tell how they will turn out. *Denise*

I still like the same books that I had as a child and I always get excited when I find an old Janet and John book. 'Why are you smelling those books?' Louis will ask in the shop. It's because there's a specific smell to a Janet and John book that doesn't exist anywhere else! *Denise*

* * *

Kicking off

I went on a five-hour flight with Jake when he was less than a year old and he didn't stop screaming from the time we got on the plane to the time we got off. I was highly embarrassed; I knew everybody hated my guts and they couldn't wait for me to get off. But what do you do? *Zoë*

I would have found a parachute and jumped out! *Carol*

If they could invent family-only planes where all hell could break loose and no one would care, I think they would do very well. It would be so great for mums to know that they're going to have nappies and milk on the plane, or colouring books, and the air stewardesses aren't going to look at you like you're something they've trodden in because your child is screaming and refuses to sit down. *Andrea*

Some years ago, I went out with this guy whose mum was quite posh and she wasn't too keen on the idea of her son going out with a single parent. Jake was three years old at the time and really naughty. We were all going out to dinner in a restaurant and I thought, do I take him? Do I leave him at home? My friend said, 'Listen, Jake is part of your life. You come as a package. Take him. Don't hide him away. If this guy wants you, he's got to take your son as well.' So I decided to take Jake along, which probably wasn't the best decision.

I bribed him with everything before we went. 'You've got to be a good boy,' I said. 'You eat all your vegetables and everything.' Well, he did as he was told. I was so proud. He ate everything; he was quiet as a little mouse.

I could see my boyfriend's mum thinking, OK, this isn't so bad. Then the chocolate pudding came. 'You've been such a good boy, haven't you?' I said to Jake.

'Yes, Mummy,' he said, and he lifted his leg and did the biggest fart you've ever, ever heard! He thought it was the funniest thing he'd ever done and literally fell off the stool laughing. And you know what? I howled. I thought, I don't care! The relationship didn't last long after that, though.   *Zoë*

I can honestly say that I don't love any one of my children more than another. But I think there are times when I do. If Jake is driving me insane, I think, I don't like you, let alone love you! And if Shane's being good, I'll say to Jake, 'Be like your brother. He's good!' But when it comes down to it, I love them all for completely different reasons. They all have fantastic traits.   *Coleen*

★ ★ ★

Gender blender

I'm from a family where there's lots of cross-gendering going on. My mother used to dress me as a boy and I'm sure I was called Dennis before they sent me for a sex change; my husband's playing a transvestite on TV; and my father's a drag artist! Somewhere along the line things have gone horribly wrong! It's quite amazing that I have two well-adjusted children.   *Denise*

As a single parent, I've had to be a mum and a dad to Jake. And he was born a fighter. In fact, somebody said to me, 'He needs to be a stuntman, your son.' So I'm very rough-and-tumble with him, because I think that's what he misses, and I do the fighting thing with him, because that's what I did with my dad. The other day, we were in the shop and Jake said to me, 'Mummy, when we go home, will you beat me up?' 'Shhhhh!' I said. 'Don't say that!' But he meant it, because I do, when we're play-fighting!   *Zoë*

My sister, who had two daughters, gave my youngest son Robbie a toy vacuum cleaner as a present. 'Why are you giving him a vacuum cleaner?' I asked. 'Because he needs to be in touch with his feminine side,' she replied.

Well, he simply looked at this vacuum and looked away. It was never even touched. He did go through a period of having a baby girl doll, for about six months, though. It had a bottle and he fed it and absolutely adored it. I thought that was great and I encouraged it. Other people reacted by saying, 'Maybe he's insecure. Obviously something is worrying him.' That struck me as a pretty negative reaction. I suppose some people may have wondered about his sexuality, but it didn't even cross my mind that I should worry. Apart from the doll episode, both my boys were very boyish. *Lynda*

* * *

Is anyone good enough for your angel?

I'm not frightened of losing my sons; I just want their girl-friends to be funny. Matthew has had a couple of girlfriends who've had no sense of humour. When they came to the house, I'd saunter into the room and walk behind them, mime cutting my throat and silently mouth 'Not funny!' at him. *Denise*

Frankly, I can't wait to get rid of my sons. I'd be out there if I could, looking for suitable girls and saying, 'Excuse me, are you free? Come here!' When my sons get married, I'll be saying, 'Bye bye!' very happily. *Lynda*

I was a bit upset this week when Louis got engaged, because he's only nine! *Denise*

How can you tell if your son is going out with someone nice? A good girlfriend will always say to her boyfriend, 'Don't you think we should go and see your mum?' *Lynda*

I think I brought Matthew up well. Obviously he doesn't expect his girlfriend Jodie to wash his clothes or cook, because his mother never did either! *Denise*

I keep schtum when it comes to my sons' girlfriends. Whatever I said, they would do the opposite. Anyway, mothers never take into account sexual chemistry. My mother might have said, 'That's a nice boy!' when in fact he was horrible. It could be a lawyer or a doctor or someone with lots of money, but if you don't fancy them, there's not a lot of point, is there? *Lynda*

* * *

The lost art of conversation

Kids need to be bored now and again. They need to be able to communicate and make conversation, which they don't, because they're always tapping away! *Carol*

I often hear that my sons have been really lovely when they've gone to somebody else's house. But in my house, they usually don't speak to me at all! As a mother, I've been guilty of it myself. They come home, they open the fridge, they grunt. 'Did you have a nice day at school?' you ask. 'Yeah.' Off they go to their room, and you don't pursue it. So sometimes you have to remind yourself to talk to your own children! *Lynda*

I worry about kids having TVs and computers in their bedrooms, because the happiest times I can remember as a child are when everybody was sat in the same room, watching family television. Even the times when we were shining shoes, while my mother was ironing, are happy memories. I think it's a shame now that as soon as you've eaten, everybody does a mass exodus to their separate places. I think we've lost the sense of family values as a result. In my day, it was only if you were really naughty that you'd go to your room, because you were sent there!
Being downstairs with the family was a treat. *Jane*

* * *

'Just one last kiss for Mummy's
little angel…MWAH'

The discipline dilemma

Jake went through a really difficult stage, from about eight to ten years old. We felt we were losing control of him. He had a terrible anger problem and when he lost his temper, he had no control over it. He used to scream and shout and smash things up. One time, out of exasperation, I said, 'Don't do that!' and smacked him on his bottom.

He immediately turned round and said, 'I could have you arrested for that.' It really shocked me. I stayed calm, but inside I thought, *he really could!*

'Yes, you could,' I explained to him, 'but it would be you they took away and put into care. I'd still be living here.'

In the end, instead of saying, 'We can't cope!' we held our hands up and said, 'We need professional help.' We had family counselling before things got completely out of control and I discovered that there were a lot of things that I thought I was doing right, but that I was actually doing wrong. Little things, like giving him choice.   *Coleen*

When a child is very disruptive at school, I'm not sure that blaming anyone will do any good. Instead, I think it's a good idea to call the parents in and work with them, alongside the child.   *Coleen*

Schools aren't allowed to discipline children anymore. Their hands are tied and children know how much power they've got, so they can abuse the system. I don't know what the answer is; I'm just glad I haven't got any of the little things!   *Carol*

If I was punished at school and I told my parents about it, they said, 'You must have deserved it!'   *Coleen*

When you start shouting at teenagers or nagging them, they just close you out. My kids now know that there's really something wrong when I'm quiet. If I say to them, 'I can't talk to you right now, because you've really upset me,' it kills them.   *Coleen*

If you're lecturing your child about something, it's much more constructive if you say, 'Look, I went through that when I was younger and this was how I dealt with it and it was a bad way of dealing with it.'   *Coleen*

My dad was lovely and gentle and funny, but he wouldn't discipline us, so my mum had to take on that role. I think it's difficult when the mum has to do the disciplining. The sad thing is that, because my husband was away a lot, I had to do exactly the same thing. I had to be Mum and Dad and I think it's really hard for a woman to take on the father's role, because you already have the mother's role. It means you become over protective. You're bound to do things wrong as a result.   *Sherrie*

I never really had any problems with the boys as teenagers. Of course, there was an element of 'Kevin and Perry' – and sometimes Jake was Kevin and Perry all in one. With me, he was shoulders down, grunting; when other people came round, he'd be, 'Yes, thank you, Mrs Patterson!' People would say, 'He's so lovely and polite!' *Really?* I'd think. He just grunts at me. But, basically, if they wanted to grunt and walk off to their rooms, I just let them get on with it.   *Coleen*

When it comes to disciplining children, I've never understood 'grounding', unless I can ground them at someone else's house. When my sons were naughty, my friend used to say, 'Just ground them for a week!' 'I don't want them in the house for a week, thank you!' I'd say. 'That's just punishing me!' So then I used to say to the boys, 'If you're not careful, I'm going to ground you – round at my friend Carol's house!'   *Coleen*

Your children can turn round to you when they're eighteen and say, 'You can't tell me what to do.' But then I can say, 'I can, because you're living in my house.' My house, my rules!   *Coleen*

* * *

Tattoos and piercings

What would I say to a mother whose sixteen-year-old daughter wants to have her tongue pierced? 'Lock her in her room and tell her she can't have it!' Beau's ten and she hasn't even had her ears pierced yet. I've said to her that when she's thirteen, I'll think about it. I suppose I'm a bit old-fashioned, but it just feels like it wasn't all that long ago when I looked at this perfectly formed little baby without any holes in her skin or anything spoiling her.   *Lisa*

I hate piercings, even though Deirdre Barlow off *Corrie* once rushed me off to Manchester to get my tummy button pierced. But that's another story. (When I was pregnant it just popped out one day and I've never seen it again!) So when my son wanted his eyebrow pierced at fifteen, I managed to put him off, thank goodness.

I also said, 'Please don't get a tattoo. I hate them!'

Around his eighteenth birthday, I wondered why he'd become 'Cardigan Boy' for a month. I questioned him about it and he showed me a tattoo on his arm. He's now got three tattoos, which he's paid for himself, and as a compromise, he says he'll have them where only he and his girlfriend can see them, which defeats the object, in a way. But it's very hard just to make a blanket ban, because they'll just rebel at that age.   *Denise*

At sixteen, Keeley wanted piercings. I decided that if you start backing up against them, they will go behind your back and do it anyway. So you make a deal, and in our case the deal was: one in each ear and a tummy piercing; no piercings anywhere on the face. I went with her and made sure it was safe. She had the tummy ring in for six months, absolutely hated it and took it out. Now she's twenty-five and hates the fact that there's a hole in her tummy button. I'm so glad she didn't go behind my back and have anything else done – and so is she!   *Sherrie*

★ ★ ★

Secrets and lies

As a parent, you think you know everything your kids are up to. You say to other parents, 'Well, your kids may be like that, but my kid would never do that.' It's only when they get to twenty that you realise how much you missed! It's just little things, like I'll say to Shane Junior, 'Why do kids always have to drink cider when they go to the park? You never did.' At that, he'll clear his throat and look slightly guilty. It's nothing major, but I really didn't think he did that!

Still, when I was a kid, there were loads of things that my parents didn't know about, so I suppose it's normal.   *Coleen*

You're not going to tell your parents what you're up to if you know it's wrong! I was absolutely terrified of my mum, not because I thought she would harm me, but because I had huge respect for her. I didn't want to let her down after she'd done such a great job bringing us up, so I never let her know what I was up to, and I was up to quite a lot of naughty things! (Smoking, mainly!) If my mum had known at the time, I can't imagine what she would have done. Later on, she knew everything, because unfortunately I was on radio and television talking about it all! *Carol*

As parents, it's impossible to keep everything hidden from your kids. Sometimes it just gets too much and it comes out. And even when you do think you've hidden it, they pick up on body language and they know what's going on, anyway. It's almost as if they're psychic. In some ways, I think that giving a kid the whole truth can be a lot better than giving them snippets of information that they go away and worry about on their own, because they tend to put two and two together and make a hundred. *Lisa*

My dad always used to say to me, 'If I ever catch you smoking, Coleen Nolan, your life won't be worth living.' So I made sure he never caught me!   *Coleen*

I think we deal with our children's problems in a different way these days. We try to entertain them by buying them gadgets or keeping them amused and occupied, rather than having quiet time at home, when you say, 'You're not right. Is there something worrying you?' Kids just disappear with their computers and all that other stuff and they just get lost in that world.   *Lisa*

My parents never wrote me a sick note and I never skived a day of school. I think it's wrong to write sick notes for children if they're not really ill. You know what? We all have to do things we don't want to do. It's called life.   *Kate*

I once wrote a sick note and gave it to one of my sons. There was half a good reason behind it, as

I recall, and I carefully composed an essay to the teacher and put it in his bag. When he came back in the evening, I said, 'Did you give him the note?'

'No, I forgot!' he said. *Hello!*

Sometimes, my boys would say, 'I don't feel well!' and I'd decide they were lying.

I'd say, 'I don't care. Let the teachers decide. You go to school and get on with it.'

Then I'd get a call an hour later: 'Your son is very, very ill and has a temperature of 102°!' *Lynda*

At school I found that it's best to write your own sick notes. I've forged a few. Sorry, Mum! *Zoë*

★ ★ ★

Career conundrum

I don't think you can actively discourage your kids from following in your footsteps. If it's something that's in them and they passionately want to do it, then you've got to encourage them. It's difficult, though. From the age of two, all Jake ever wanted was to be on the stage. He didn't go through those normal phases of wanting to be a policeman, a fireman or a footballer. I don't think it would have made any difference if I'd said, 'No you can't go into show business; I don't want you to.' It's his passion; it's in his blood, as they say. All Shane Junior ever wanted to be was a footballer and he was a great footballer. He had trials for lots of teams. But then at eighteen he decided he wanted to sing and now the two of them are in the business. People say, 'I wouldn't want them to be in show business. It's a hard life.' And it is. But it's also a great life, really. There are so many ups and downs. *Coleen*

When Keeley was young, she was in *Coronation Street* with me. She was in Better Buys when I met Reg! She was there most days, with her 'mum' and her 'dad' and she loved it. The only thing she didn't like was the time Reg had to kiss me. She ran the full length of Better Buys and shouted, 'Get off my mummy!' *Sherrie*

There's a big difference between encouraging your children and pushing them. *Denise*

Forget fame and riches; all that really matters to a mother is that her child is happy. *Sherrie*

It's about encouraging your children to follow their dreams, whatever they may be. What you want for your kids is for them to jump out of bed every day, because they're going off to do something they really, really want to do. *Kate*

Matthew's into music. We've encouraged him and he's doing really well. As he knows, I'm supporting him mainly because I want my MTV crib in Beverly Hills one day, when he's a rock star! *Denise*

* * *

Guiding influence

When Shane Junior reached sixteen and realised that his dream of becoming a footballer wasn't going to come true, or not in a way that would give him a good living, he went through a stage of not knowing what he wanted to do.

At that point, he started doing nothing. I asked him, 'What do you want to do?'

'I don't know,' he kept saying.

Waterloo... Wa... Wa... Wa.. Wa....

This isn't exactly what Maddie had in mind when
she took her Mum to see *Mamma Mia...!*'

'Well, until you do know, you need to get a job,' I said, 'because you're not living off me until you make your mind up, love.' And he did. I would never force my children to do anything they didn't want to do, but I would always want them to do something.

Jake knew what he wanted to do, so when it came to his GCSE year, he said, 'I don't see the point in doing GCSEs, because they're not going to be beneficial to anything I want to do.'

So I said, 'You have to stay at school anyway, by law, so why not do your exams to the best of your ability? You might not want them now, but twenty years down the line they may come in handy. And the fact is, you'll be proud enough to say, "I got them."'

'How many did you get?' he threw back at me, of course. 'That's the one regret of my life,' I told him. 'Even though I haven't needed them, I would love to sit here and say, "I passed eight O Levels." Just to say I got them! I'd be really proud of myself.'   *Coleen*

* * *

Kids in training

I'm not paying my kid to clean his bedroom. No one pays me to clean the kitchen!   *Coleen*

It's your responsibility as a mother to send your son off to the woman who he'll share a life and home with, knowing that actually homes don't run themselves. 'It's not a hotel, mate.' It's really important.   *Kate*

You can't just let kids think that they can be given everything for nothing. We didn't get pocket money, but we still did all the chores. One of our chores was to lay and clear the table. We used to put a second tablecloth over the tablecloth, to keep it clean. After a meal, my mum would say, 'Could someone go and shake the tablecloth?' We thought it was hilarious to fold it up with all the crumbs in it, so that when she took it out to put on the table, the crumbs would tumble out! We'd really get told off. *Carol*

* * *

When things go wrong . . .

I went through a period of having a very bad time with my ex. I remember one terrible row when we were screaming at one another. It was awful. Keeley was only eight and in the end she shouted, 'Please stop! Stop, please!' It shocked me. Suddenly I realised what I'd done. She was taking it all in! It was so selfish of us to scream and shout at each other in front of an eight-year-old, but because of the stress I was under, it never occurred to me what I was doing. *Sherrie*

I've been around rowing parents who use the kids as ammunition against one another. I look at them and

I think, who are the children here? It's the grown-ups who are acting like kids. Grow up!   *Carol*

Kids are very astute. They work things out for themselves as they grow older and they deal with things in their own way. So if you're divorced or separated, you don't have to slag their dad off or try and sway their thoughts or make them love you more. Just try to be honest when they ask a question, without apportioning blame.   *Coleen*

My father left when I was very young. I don't remember that much about it, to be honest, and I don't remember asking. Maybe I did, but I don't remember what my mum said, so it obviously hasn't had that much of an effect. All credit to my mother, I never heard her say anything negative about my dad – not once. I had to prise it out of her in later life. 'Why didn't you ever say anything?' I asked her. 'I had to leave you lot to make up your own minds,' she said. She thought that there was no point in trying to influence us, because it might drive us towards him.   *Carol*

When you go to a family party, and your kids are exposed to people they know very, very well who change when they're drinking alcohol, I think it's really frightening for them. When I was a kid, I always became very scared of people I knew that were drunk. I just wanted to get away from them. It's something we have to be aware of, as adults, and quite often people aren't. *Kate*

★ ★ ★

Sport and exercise

Even though I'm not very competitive or sporty, I hate the fact that schools have taken the competition out of sports day and things like that. The fact is, life is about competition, and healthy competitiveness is a good thing. With my kids, I'd rather they did better in their effort grades than their achievement grades, because all that matters is that they've tried their best. *Denise*

★ ★ ★

Weight debate

Instead of concentrating on weight, kids should be taught why they should be eating good food. It's not just about whether it will make you slim or fat; it should be about making you healthy. You'll have lovely hair and lovely teeth; you'll be strong and have more energy to run faster and play more. Small children will respond far better to that kind of advice than to warnings about weight.   *Coleen*

When we were at school, there used to be cooking classes. They don't exist anymore, but that's how we learnt about food and about the fat and sugar that's in food. Children today should be taught what food is made up of and what it does.   *Sherrie*

If the parents aren't living healthily, then what hope is there for the kids? I have seen overweight kids out in the street and normally following behind them are Mr and Mrs Overweight. It makes you want to say, 'Step back from the cake, fatty!'   *Coleen*

I think a lot of kids now who have self-esteem issues inherit them from their parents. Paranoid mothers who are always on diets are bound to pass on their body-image issues to their daughters, aren't they?   *Carol*

★ ★ ★

Holiday fun

I love being on holiday with Louis, but I'm not very good at 'pool fun'. I think it's a paradox. 'Come on, Mummy, jump in and let me swim under your legs!' I hate all that. My *hair*! I never do the water slides and I swim with my neck sticking out because I don't like to get water on my face. But that's maybe something to do with the fact that my dad never swam. The old photographs of me and my dad having pool fun show him with armbands on!   *Denise*

I don't think I ever saw my mum get in the pool unless it reached over 100° and she needed to dip her ankles in to cool down. She was almost like, 'Don't talk to me, I'm reading.' There's nothing wrong with that, but we were young and childlike and wanted to play. My dad was like that too, so they actually worked it out very well. I used to quite like a sunbathe and he'd tap me and say, 'Get that Walkman off. Come on, a bit of crazy golf will be great. Let's build something!' I'd doze off and he'd tap me again. 'Can you see your brother? No? I've buried him!' He was brilliant and he's still the same today. *Kate*

The only problem with your child making a friend on holiday is that sometimes you get saddled with the parents of the friend. When Matthew was little, he made friends with a gorgeous little boy, but the parents! 'Oh, Denise,' they kept saying, 'when we get back, you've got to come round. We've got a lovely mock Tudor!' *Denise*

When I was a kid, it was either a tent or a caravan when we went on holiday. And my mother never went without me, because she knew that if she did, she'd have to give my dad some fun! *Jane*

Sex

It's one thing *doing* it (and that's not always the exhilaratingly saucy thrillfest it should be after an eighteen-hour day of clearing up baby sick and changing nappies) but it's something else altogether *explaining* it. When your kids ask those difficult questions, do you try to distract them with pictures of fluffy bunnies? Or bore them senseless with a detailed lesson in biology? What did your mum tell you? (Or not tell you!) And when and how did you break it to your parents that you weren't a little girl anymore?

* * *

The birds and the bees

I never understood what a bird does with a bee
and my mother never explained it to me properly. The bee would sting the bird, wouldn't it?
And I used to wonder, if a little bird pecked my
hand, would that make me pregnant?   *Sherrie*

I don't think you necessarily have to sit down with
your kids and say, 'OK, let's talk about the birds and
the bees,' because that might get a bit embarras-
ing for them. On the other hand, I grew up with
parents who didn't talk about these things and I had
to find out through friends and magazines.

With my boys, at each stage that they felt worried about
something or inquisitive, they would come up and ask
me. Even at the moments when I thought, *oh, I'm a
bit embarrassed about this*, I didn't let them know. I just
went ahead and answered the question.   *Coleen*

I remember my mother trying to sit me down and tell me about the facts of life, but I didn't want to listen. I just wanted to put my hands up to my ears and go, 'La la la!' *Carol*

When it comes to the birds and the bees, I think a mother should tell her daughter 'things' and a father should tell his son 'things'. Because a woman doesn't know what to do with those things that boys have – the ins and outs, ups and downs – so she can't tell a boy what that's for. With a girl, we women know our bits, don't we? We all know what they do. But I can't see how a father would know what a woman's bits do. *Sherrie*

My son Jake used to have his own little words for things, including the parts of the body, which was really cute. But one day he went to school and told the teacher, 'Mummy's got somebody coming round today. She's having her flower waxed!' *Zoë*

'How did it get in your tummy Mummy? Did you eat it?'
'Well...Daddy said hello to Mummy in a special way...!'

I'm a farmer's daughter and I reckon that all children should spend time on a farm to understand the cycle of life.   *Lynda*

* * *

Sealed with a kiss

I was watching a wildlife programme with Ciara when she was seven and there was a bit with two seals mating. Ciara asked, 'So how does the seed get to the egg?'

I said, 'Well, because Daddy gives it to Mummy.' I thought, *aren't I grown-up and mature?*

Then she asked, 'How does Daddy give it to Mummy?'

I said, 'I'm sure there's someone at the door,' and I legged it into the office, where Ray was. 'I'm having a parenting moment!' I told him. 'I don't know how to deal with it.'

Shane asked me when he was about ten or eleven and I explained it all very maturely. Jake was a bit younger when he asked; I went into a long explanation that lasted about twenty minutes and at the end he said, 'Can I have an ice lolly?' He just couldn't be bothered! So I felt Ciara was too young at seven.   *Coleen*

* * *

Virgin on the ridiculous

My parents never gave me a birds and bees talk. I just had to find out about it for myself. I think I pretty much always knew about sex, but for ages I didn't know what a virgin was. I didn't know what the word meant and I was very embarrassed that I didn't.

Walking along the seafront with my friend Christine, when we were twelve or thirteen – and I'll remember this day forever – I said something like, 'If you had to describe what

a virgin was, how would you sort of put it into words?'
'Well, somebody who hasn't had sex!' she said.

'Exactly! That's just how I would put it,' I said quickly.   *Denise*

The other day, Ciara asked Ray and me an embarrassing question: 'Mum, Dad, what exactly is a virgin?' She had been watching an old video of Madonna singing 'Like a Virgin'.

Ray started typing on his computer, pretending he was completely deaf and hadn't heard her. I thought, I don't think she's old enough at nine to know exactly what a virgin is, but I have to give her some explanation. So I said, 'Well, I'm not one!' No, I didn't, really! I said, 'It's a young lady before she has a boyfriend.'

Now, I'm a little bit worried now that she'll go into class and say, 'Miss, Orla's not a virgin cos she's got a boyfriend! And she's only nine!'   *Coleen*

★ ★ ★

Mummy's little girl

My first ever TV role was in *The Misfit*, a series starring an actor called Ronnie Fraser, who was renowned for being wild and drinking quite a lot. He's dead now, God bless him. One day, we'd all been out to lunch and he rang my mum and said, 'Hello, it's Ronnie Fraser here. I want to take your daughter to Paris for dinner.'

'Really?' my mum said. 'But don't be so silly. How will she get home?' *Lynda*

* * *

Not under my roof!

I was about eighteen when a boy first stayed at my mum's house. We didn't have a spare room or a put-you-up, so I said, 'He can just come in with me. We won't do anything.' (That old chestnut!)

But you can't exactly surrender to the moment in your parents' house, can you? I think my mum had some idea that we might have a kiss and a cuddle, but she didn't really want to go there. Parents usually know what's going on, but they turn a blind eye.   *Lisa*

When I was living with my second husband, before we were married, I took him home for the weekend. We'd been going out together for quite a while and I said to Mum, 'Can we move the other single bed into my room?'

'Yes,' she said. 'Your dad won't notice; he won't go in your room.'

But Dad caught us on the stairs with the single bed. 'Not in my house, you're not!' he thundered.

'Oh, come along!' Mum said.

'No, she can do what she likes in her house, but not here!'
So we never did. I had to respect that it was his house.

It's the opposite with my boys. Whatever they're
doing, I like them to do it under my roof, so I can
keep an eye on things. I don't mean with a glass
to the wall, or anything, though!   *Lynda*

* * *

Playing the innocent

When I was nineteen, my boyfriend at the time
and I were about to go away to separate universities.
Because we both lived with our parents, we booked
a B&B for the night. I lied about where I was going
and said, 'I'm going to stay at my friend Claire's.'

But then I got caught out, driving back
from the wrong side of town the next

morning. 'Why were you coming back from that part of Chester?' my parents asked.

I came completely clean. I said to Mum, 'I don't want to lie to you. I was in this B&B . . . We love each other and we're going away . . .'

'I really wish you hadn't told me,' she said. 'I understand what you're doing, but I really didn't need to know! It's too much information.' *Andrea*

My sister and I were brought up by the strictest dad. Because he was so strict, I never wanted him to know anything about my boyfriends, even when I was twenty-four and seeing the man who went on to become my husband. One night we all went out to dinner and my boyfriend and I had booked a hotel. Even then, I felt I had to protect my dad. When he asked, 'Where are you staying tonight?' and Paul said, 'We're staying in a hotel,' I immediately said, 'I don't feel very well, Dad,' because I wanted him to think that I wouldn't be having sex that night! I wanted him to think that I was just going to go to sleep when I got back to the hotel. I was twenty-four years old! It never ends, does it?   *Zoë*

I still don't discuss sex with my mum. I don't know if other people my age do. I guess they would. When I got pregnant with Beau, I remember thinking, *now my mum knows I've had sex!* I'm not only telling her that I'm pregnant; I'm telling her that I'm having sexual intercourse with my boyfriend at the same time.   *Lisa*

★ ★ ★

Sex after babies

Often the biggest threat to a man is when a woman has a baby. People talk about postnatal depression and the effect on women, which is great, but not enough is done to help men understand that women can love and love and love; the more people they are asked to love, the more they do love. Men can't understand it. They think that if a woman loves her children deeply, she can't love her husband as much.

It's probably because, much as men love their children, they don't love them in that all-consuming way. So it's important for women to include them at the same time as experiencing this all-consuming love for a baby. Unfortunately, that can often mean being sexual and two months after the baby is born, you might have stitches and not feel very sexual. So many women have said to me, 'He's so selfish! It's the last thing on my mind.'

'Well, try and make it the first thing on your mind,' I've said. 'If you don't want to, just get going and your body will take over. It doesn't have to be the best sex ever, but he needs it to make him feel secure and for the good of the relationship.'

From the outside, it can easily feel excluding to look at this amazing aura of love surrounding a mother and child. Also, who is to say that seeing you breastfeeding doesn't bring something back for a man, an animal memory of his own experiences as a baby?   *Lynda*

* * *

Switch on/switch off

When you've got young kids, it's often a quickie. I've said it before and I'll say it again: it just depends how long an episode of *Peppa Pig* it is. If it's on satellite, they'll sometimes show three episodes in a row, one after another, so you get about twenty minutes!   *Andrea*

I've got a switch-off mode when my daughter is around. I've got used to switching from sexy-partner mode into mother mode and never the twain shall meet!   *Lisa*

It's difficult to have sex with kids in the house, especially teenagers. Unfortunately, they don't stay in their cots at that age!   *Coleen*

A two-hour, child-free gap means different things to men and women. He sees it as an opportunity for sex, while the woman is thinking, 'How much housework can I get done before the baby wakes up?' *Denise*

Dads and Relationships

It's all too easy to overlook the importance of dads. Sure, they don't get pregnant or give birth; OK, they don't breast-feed. True, they're often not all that keen on changing nappies ... but they're great at, er, flying kites! So although the role of the father may not always be a practical one, dads still exert plenty of influence, especially on their daughters. But should they play a defined role? Or can dads be mums and vice versa, depending on the circumstances? And should you put your relationship above your children?

What is it that dads do, again?   *Sherrie*

Put the bins out!   *Andrea*

* * *

Doting dads

Tim loved it when I was pregnant. Some men don't like the look or the feel of a woman in pregnancy, but he embraced the whole thing. There are men who don't find women sexually attractive when they're pregnant, whereas I often wished that Tim wouldn't find me sexually attractive, so I could get a break! No, but seriously, he loved both my pregnancies and was very supportive. He had to be, because there were some real mood swings going on there! *Denise*

There is something about a 'real' man holding a baby that is so sexy and so endearing, isn't there? *Lynda*

My father was unconditionally loving. He loved me beyond belief. It wouldn't have mattered if I'd killed fifty people, he'd still have said, 'Don't worry, we will find a way out of this. I'll sort it.' *Sherrie*

After the whole family forgot last year, Tracey was a little overwhelmed at this year's offerings.

Ray loved every minute that I was pregnant. He was at every scan and doctor's appointment and wanted to feel every kick. He was there for the entire birth and he did everything for the first ten days. I didn't even change a nappy. When I had Ciara, I practically went straight back to work, so he was the main parent for the first three months. I think it hurts him that she sobs when I'm going away, because he does so much for her. But that bond with the mother is so strong, isn't it? *Coleen*

★ ★ ★

Keeping up with the kids

It took Tim quite a long time to come round to the idea that I was pregnant for the second time. He was nearly fifty and he said, 'I'm going to be sixty-eight when I take him for his first pint!' He wouldn't have chosen to have another child then, but now of course he wouldn't swap Louis for the world. *Denise*

It's great, because Shane still comes up to Ray and me and says, 'We're going out. Do you want to come out with us?' and we'll go out with him. But I can't imagine Ciara saying the same thing in another ten years, when I'm nearly sixty.   *Coleen*

Well, it doesn't matter, because I'll be taking her out!   *Denise*

Yes, you'll still be going out. Oldest swinger in town, you are.   *Coleen*

'Come with Nana, Ciara!'   *Denise*

Don't you think it's better to have a good father for a short amount of time than a rubbish father for the whole of your life? There are some people who have their children very young who are terrible, terrible fathers.   *Denise*

One of the reasons Mr Spain asked me to marry him was because he knew it was too late for me to have any more children, thank goodness!   *Lynda*

Would you like a little Mr Spain? *Carol*

No, thank you. Not at all. *Lynda*

* * *

Mum vs. Dad

My mum was the one that screamed and shouted and chased us with a bamboo cane and yet my dad was the one we were scared of. It's really weird, because he very rarely smacked us. He didn't have to. He would just stand there and look at you and you would die a thousand deaths. *Coleen*

There are certain things Matthew will come and talk to me about, not because he feels he couldn't talk to his dad about it, but because I'm his mum. So if he and his girlfriend are having a problem or if he's upset about something, he comes and sits on the end of the bed and talks to me. He's a very sensitive kid. Tim would be as equally as supportive and helpful to him; it's just that I'm his mum. That's the way it works.   *Denise*

I'm absolutely disgusted when I read that a woman has left her husband and kids and gone off with another man. When a man does it, I write him off as a b******, but when a woman does it, I'm much more horrified. How could she leave her kids? I don't get it.

If I went off with another man, I'd have to take my children! Or at least work out a way to see them. Yet some women just walk away and don't look back. I cannot get my head round that. I always think there must be some mental illness involved, but I don't think that with a man. I just think, oh well, that's a man for you, shirking his responsibilities. Off he goes with a younger model!

And when a man says, 'Couldn't be dealing with kids; not interested,' I'll say, 'You don't know what you're missing.' But when a woman says, 'I can't stand kids. I'd hate to have kids,' I always think there's something wrong there – and there is!   *Coleen*

Role refusals

Tim and I don't really have defined roles at all; at least, they're a lot less defined than they are for a lot of couples. The nature of our work means that sometimes Tim is busy and I have to hold the fort at home, which is when the children either starve or get take-outs. At other times, I'm away, so Tim has to be mother, father and chef.

I'm very lucky that I can go away and work knowing that Tim is at home. I don't mean that everything will get done; it won't. Men don't multitask very well. So the dead light bulbs won't have been changed and we'll be in blackout when I get back, but at least the children will be fed. Tim doesn't do DIY. He doesn't see things that need doing like that. It does bug me sometimes, but I'd much prefer him to be a good nurturer while I'm away.   *Denise*

I was mother and father to Keeley. There was never any discussion: I made the decisions; I chose the schools; I picked out the clothes; I went to sports days and parents' meetings; I took her on holiday. He never came to a nativity play and I never expected him to.

Sometimes her dad was there and sometimes not. I don't want to be unfair to him, because I'm sure he loved her, but he didn't necessarily want children; it was not a world he wanted. So she was mine from the day she was born. That was the end of the story. I know it sounds strange, but it's the way our life was. I guess that's why I didn't have any more children, because he was not a child person.   *Sherrie*

You have to train men to be domestic, God love 'em. Before we moved in together, I wouldn't have expected to go and clean Ed's house just as I wouldn't have expected him to come and clean mine. My mother cleaned mine, obviously!   *Jane*

I'm always saying to Ray, 'Don't die, because I don't know how to do my tax return.' At the same time, he's saying, 'Don't die, because I don't know where Ciara's uniform is.' We each have our jobs and we do them!   *Coleen*

* * *

Father complex

I suggested to my father once that maybe he shouldn't have been married. There are certain men who don't suit marriage; they should live their lives unfettered because they are not the type that can take on commitment. Women don't live those types of lives, do we? We're different because we are more likely to have commitments to anchor us, and that's our choice. Ever since I was a child I have been aware of the need for responsibility and determination, forever creating more responsibility for myself because I was so driven.   *Sherrie*

* * *

Daddy's little girl

I had my first proper boyfriend when I was seventeen and he was twenty-one. He was lovely and his name was Darren. But my dad decided that he was too old to be going out with me. It was crazy, because if he'd thought about it, this guy was a perfect gentleman who always opened doors for me. When I said, 'No, I'm not legal to drink yet, so I'll have a Coca Cola, thank you,' he never said, 'Go on, get drunk! Your dad's not here!' like other boys might have done. (Not that I would have known, because I'd never been out with anyone else!)

Anyway, my dad said, 'No, he's too old. I don't like it.' So I had to break up with him. I only went out with him three times! My dad ruled the roost and I was far too obedient. Just look where it got me!   *Andrea*

Oh, my poor parents! I used to take some shockers back. My dad used to out-sit me. He would never go to bed until they'd gone. Ed, the guy I'm engaged to now, was in a rock and roll band in those days. He once turned up at our house in the middle of the summer wearing skin-tight leather trousers and a vest. He had really long blond hair and a gold earring. My dad thought, *oh God, what's she brought home now?* But he took him up the allotment and had a fag with him anyway.

A little later, my mother said, 'Go and tell them the dinner's out.' So I went off to meet them as they were walking back. I actually laughed out loud when I saw them – there was Ed, 6ft 4ins, in his leather trousers, towering over my little dad in his work pants with his onions in his hand. I thought, that's a sight for sore eyes! That night Ed slept on the couch – wink wink – or so my parents thought! *Jane*

I remember my dad once saying, 'I can't believe I've got six daughters and not one of you has married a millionaire!' Ultimately, your parents want you to be with somebody who can look after you. They'd like you never to have any worries for the rest of your life. Of course, my sisters and I met a lot of millionaires, but we always went for love, never for money. *Coleen*

When I was twenty-one, I moved in with a boyfriend and I don't think my dad approved. I was surprised that he never said anything, because if you stepped out of line with my dad, you knew about it. He was very disciplinarian. But he said nothing at all. That's what really affected me, the fact that he didn't say, 'That's great, we'll come and visit you.' He let me do it but he didn't approve and I just wanted him to say something. *Zoë*

★ ★ ★

Dad puts his foot down

I thought smoking looked glamorous on the old films and I used to go down to the end of the garden and smoke tea leaves! I rolled them up in a bit of paper and spat them out; it was disgusting. My mum and dad didn't really smoke, but my dad was a pilot and he used to come back with these untipped cigarettes called State Express 555, so I went on to them next. 'Come here!' my dad said, one day. He called me over to a huge cigar and a bucket. 'Now,' he said. 'You're going to smoke the cigar and then you're going to be sick in the bucket.' So I smoked the cigar and I was sick in the bucket – and I still carried on smoking! *Lynda*

When we were younger, my sisters and I weren't allowed boys from school at our birthday parties; it was all girls. For my older sisters, that was a rule that extended past teenage years! But by the time it got to me, my dad seemed to have given up. I think he thought, 'You know what? She's the eighth kid; I don't care!' *Coleen*

★ ★ ★

Father first

I have never forgotten an incident that took place when I had just left drama school and was starting out on my professional career. I was at home for a few days and one evening, from the top of the stairs, I heard talking in the kitchen. As I came down, I realised that it was my father crying. I was devastated and panic struck me, because if somebody like my father was crying, then things were really bad. It turned out that our farm was going to be eaten up by runway number three of the proposed Wycombe Airport. All we would be left with was a house at the edge of the runway, so Dad felt that his only option was to go into contracting out farm equipment, like combine harvesters and tractors. However, in order to do this he had to buy the machinery – and a combine harvester was probably the same price as a Rolls Royce.

As I listened outside the kitchen door, I heard Dad saying tearfully to my mum, 'We just don't have enough money! The numbers don't add up and I don't know what we're going to do. If I could just get the money to buy one combine harvester to rent out, that would be all we need to get started.'

Shortly after this, I got a part in the telly series, *General Hospital*, and I gave Dad the first £500 I earned, which helped towards buying his first combine harvester. I was so grateful to be able to pay him back in a small way for everything that he and my mum had ever done for me. It got him off the ground.   *Lynda*

Like all kids, when we were out shopping, I used to say to my mum, 'Can I have that? I want that!'

One day, my mum said, 'Darling, yes, you can have that toy, but your daddy won't be able to have his tea. Which would you rather? I can buy it for you, no problem, but when your daddy comes in from work, he won't have anything to eat.'

I said, 'No, my daddy needs to eat.' It gave me an idea of the value of things and made me realise that there wasn't enough money to buy everything.   *Jane*

There used to be a character in the *Viz* comic called 'Competitive Dad' and I'm sure that Tim was the prototype for him. For Matthew's twenty-first birthday, I arranged for him and nine friends to go speed-carting. It's only for over eighteens and you have to be quite strong to do it. Anyway, a couple of nights before they went, Tim said to me, 'I don't think I should get on that speed-cart, flower.'

'Why not?' I asked. 'Matthew would love you to go.'

'The thing is, I'll win!' Tim said.

Guess who came last! Apparently he got knocked off, into the tyres. Gutted, he was! He even tries to compete with me in acting roles – and I'm a woman. I'm sure that's why he took the part of the transvestite in *Benidorm*, just to prove that he can play a woman!   *Denise*

* * *

The ups and downs of marriage

I know people who have created what they think is a perfect life, with a husband and a baby. Then they suddenly think, maybe I've done this too soon. It's the wrong person. I'm moving on. They separate and think, isn't it great? We've got our single lives back! We can each have the kid every other weekend. I object to that.

There's this endless pursuit of selfish happiness and some-times people give up way too easily. I think it's too easy to get married and too easy to get divorced.   *Carol*

These days, it seems that marriage is disposable as far as some people are concerned. But when children are involved, you can't just give up at the first obstacle. Don't stay if you're desperately unhappy, of course. I wouldn't recommend that at all. But there's a lot you can work through and if you have children you have a responsibility to try and stay together.   *Denise*

I was married for twenty-five years, seventeen of which were desperately unhappy. But I stayed because I had a child and I felt it was my duty to stay. I stayed for all the right reasons and it was wrong, because if we had split when we were meant to, Keeley and I would have had another life, he would have had another life and we would have found happiness somewhere else.   *Sherrie*

Tim and I have always said that we wouldn't stay together just because of the children, but I think that having children makes you work harder at staying together. My youngest is very used to us being apart, so the actual physical separation wouldn't be that apparent to him. For a lot of his life, Mummy has had a flat in Maidstone or Daddy's had a house in London, because of our work. He thinks we've got houses all over the globe! So really that side of it would be quite easy for him to adjust to. That's what I mean when I say we don't stay together for the children, but I'm glad that we have. I would find it quite hard to go and see Matty's band, or Louis in something at school, separately from Tim. There's something about the history and the bonds that I like.   *Denise*

My parents met when they were fifteen and sixteen; they've been together ever since and they're still massively in love with each other. They were, and still are, how a married couple should be. I met my ex-husband when I was at school and all I ever wanted to do, and tried to do, was to emulate their marriage. I thought that if you hit a rocky patch, you just keep working at it, because that's what marriage is. You battle through and love will prevail. It took a long time to admit to myself that, actually, this isn't working. I'm not going to have what my mum and dad have. And it destroyed me.   *Andrea*

I always say that the marriage vows were invented when people died aged thirty-five. You were only meant to do ten years max. No idiot would have suggested to people that it was supposed to go on this long!   *Denise*

★ ★ ★

A balancing act

I think you should make your husband number one. Not all the time, but sometimes your man needs you as much as your children do. I struggle with this, because I instinctively put Beau right at the top of the list when I'm busy. There are times when I've not even registered that Paul needs a conversation or to share something with me. But at the end of the day, the kids fly the coop and you're left with your partner – hopefully – so you should prioritise them sometimes.   *Lisa*

Shouldn't your children be number one on your list of priorities, because they're not able to care for themselves?   *Kate*

Kids of a certain age know that Dad needs a bit
of attention. If they see you come home and go
straight to your partner and show your partner love
and kindness, it makes them feel secure.   *Lisa*

I'm always a bit suspicious of people who say, 'My
marriage comes first and then my kids.'   *Kate*

I've seen a vast change from my parents' day to today. When
we were kids, we had to fit in with our parents' lives. We
were in bed for seven and then they had their time together.
But now everything seems to revolve around the children
of the family and the parents drift slightly apart.   *Jane*

Kids need to know that Mum and Dad are rock solid and everything is fine there. It makes them feel secure. *Lisa*

I've seen women who live their lives through their children and they completely forget about the husband. You have to find a balance. *Jane*

There's an old adage: I'd kill for my husband and die for my kids. Mine is: I'd kill my husband and die for my kids. (I'm only teasing!) *Denise*

I tried to have a baby for eight years, so when I had Keeley, she was the love of my life. She still is the love of my life. Therefore, I did the unforgivable and forgot the man in my life. So I'm always saying to Keeley, 'Just remember you love Simon and what you had with Simon before you had Oliver.' I'm probably not the right person to say it, because my marriage was breaking down anyway, but nevertheless, Keeley was it. There was nobody else for me. I forgot the marriage altogether. *Sherrie*

'How about you and I discuss some
extra-curricular activities of our own?',
Roxanne said to a bewildered Mr. Mackenzie.

You often see women neglecting their husbands for the sake of their children. I'm sure I wouldn't do that. A lot of people might say, 'Well, you're going to be married to Mark and he's quite young, so you don't have to make a choice, because it's all rolled into one!'   *Carol*

★ ★ ★

Mums and Work

Modern motherhood is a balancing act, especially if you work. At home, your kids are their usual demanding selves; at work, your colleagues are their usual demanding selves. Sometimes it's hard to know who's the bigger baby! So how do you find an equilibrium between career and motherhood? Can you do it all and have it all, or is it just a question of living by your wits, hour by hour? Which comes first, kids or career? And can maternity leave ever be long enough?

My advice to any busy working mum would be to try and take an hour a day, or an hour every couple of days, to think about yourself or do something for yourself. But I know how hard it is. You just don't do it, do you?   *Coleen*

* * *

Priorities

A lot of couples can't have a mortgage now without both of them working. It's blimmin' hard work! So if you choose to have a career and children, you have to understand how hard it's going to be.   *Lynda*

The workplace needs to make life easier for women. They should have crèches so that they don't have to rush off at three o'clock to pick the kids up from school.   *Coleen*

I don't think you can do it all. If you have a family, then your first priority should be the family.   *Jane*

I know quite a lot of people who have children and then actively pursue a career. Nothing changes in their life and I don't really understand that. I look at them and think, why did you have children when your main focus is still you and your career, rather than your kids?   *Carol*

I think it works both ways. Women often go back to work because their family is their priority. They work hard because they have to – they have a family to look after. (Single women work hard, too, of course.) It's often said that employees who are mothers are always worried about their children and frequently leave work early. But they are also the employees who will hang on to their jobs for dear life, because they've got a family to think of.   *Coleen*

My mum had to work, because we had no money. So she took a job in a pub. It wasn't what she wanted to do, but it was perfect for us, because in those days, pubs opened at 11 am and shut at 3 pm, which fitted in with school time. There was absolutely no way she would have given us keys; she was always there when we left for school and when we got home from school. I think that's very important, especially with so many mums being out to work now, often, to sustain a lifestyle that they don't need to sustain. People work to get big houses and big cars and they think that's more important. 'I'm doing it for my kids,' they say. No, the kids don't care. You're doing it because you want to live in a big house and have a big car. But something's got to give. *Carol*

★ ★ ★

Should maternity leave last longer?

You should have the choice to take a year if you really want it. Most women don't; they return either part-time or full-time during that period. But I think it's fabulous that we have that option. *Kate*

Instead of increasing the length of mater-nity leave, I'd rather see more crèches in the workplace to make it easier for women to take their children to work with them. *Lynda*

Not everyone has to take a year off, but I don't understand the thinking behind the people who want to take that choice away from women, especially when we've fought so hard to be taken seriously on that front. If a woman is fantastic in her job and her role, then an employer should want to have her back at any point during the fifty-two weeks she is legally allowed to be away. *Kate*

I didn't have maternity leave; I had to work to survive, even though I would have loved to stay at home. I think it's unrealistic. Nobody legislated for me or my mother or my mother's mother. *Lynda*

But isn't it great that they now have? *Kate*

I don't think things have changed. Ultimately, it will always be up to women to decide how far they want to go up the career ladder – or whether they want to stay at home. The people who want to work and go to the top make sacrifices and suffer and the people who want to stay at home, quite rightly, stay at home. *Lynda*

I haven't had any babies, but can I have a year off, with pay? What about me? I think it's really unfair!   *Carol*

Apparently, much of your character and personality is formed as a baby in your first year. But sometimes, to be honest, maternity leave is more about the mum's needs than the baby's. I think children need you more when they get older. My twenty-year-old needs me around more at the moment than he did as a small baby, because babies are alright as long as they've got some food and some loving arms. However, mums feel that they want to be with their newborn child and that's understandable.   *Denise*

When we're talking about rights and choices, I think men are horribly overlooked in this area. It's disgraceful that men only get two weeks paternity leave. They should be given far more flexibility and options. You know what? When you've just given birth, you need more than two weeks' help around the house.   *Kate*

Most men would take on another seven jobs to get out of the house after two weeks with a new baby!   *Denise*

After I said on *Loose Women* that I wouldn't give up my seat on the tube to a pregnant woman, I am now hated by pregnant women and women with children all over the country. So I would just like to put it on the record that I think that pregnant women and women with children should never have to work. They should get ten years maternity leave – is that enough? They should have free travel, free clothes and free holidays; there should be red carpets everywhere they walk and a buggy lane exclusively for them on the pavements. They're heroes, they're saints. Everything about women with babies is fantastic. I love them all!   *Carol*

★ ★ ★

Under pressure

It's acceptable for women to do more now, but I
think there's also more pressure on us.   *Coleen*

Women used to give up their careers when they had kids
in order to bring the kids up. Now there's a lot of pressure on women – and they've put it on themselves, more
than anything – to do everything, have everything and
be good at everything. But you can't be good at everything and you've got to make your choices.   *Carol*

* * *

Independent woman

Perhaps because of her own experience of marriage, my
mother has always said: 'Make sure you have enough
money to look after yourself.' In her day, you couldn't leave
a marriage if you were unhappy, because where would

It had only been 3 weeks since her caesarean but
Justine was determined to shift her baby weight.

you go? You would have been frowned upon for leaving and you couldn't go out there and get a job like we can now. So I've always been the type of woman to go out and earn my own money, so that I could stand on my own two feet and not need a man to take care of me. *Jane*

* * *

Mums missing out

Working mums carry a lot of guilt. Not so long ago, something happened that is now referred to in our house as 'Duckgate', so called because Louis was playing a duck in *Wind in the Willows*. I now know that there is no such character in *Wind in the Willows*, but he and a group of other children had to do a little duck dance all the same. Anyway, to cut a long story short, I was in a television drama at the time and I asked for permission to go to the play. They said yes. But when you're in a TV drama the schedule changes all the time, so the next minute they changed their minds and said I couldn't go. Then they rang and said, 'We've moved heaven and earth. You can go and see Louis be a duck.'

So I told Louis that I could go and see him be a duck. But on the day of the play, the producers said, 'We're so sorry. We've had to change that scene. You can't go.'

'Just watch me!' I said. 'At 5.30 pm I'm walking out this door to go and watch him be a duck.' Admittedly, his duck dance lasted for 3.4 seconds and I couldn't see him from the back, but the fact is, he knew that I was there.

With Matthew, I missed quite a big gig that he had at Newcastle not so long ago. I felt gutted, but he said, 'Part of me was relieved, Mum, because remember the last time you came to see a gig and you'd had a couple of glasses of wine? You ran on stage and pulled my trousers up!' *Denise*

My mum and dad always missed parents' evening and sports day, because they were working, God bless them. Every sports day, I'd come out thinking, I bet they've surprised me. But they never did.

I don't love my parents any less for it, but I remember the feeling of disappointment, so when I had my children, I became a bit obsessive about not missing anything. There was one time when I was offered two days' work and it was really quite lucrative. My manager said, 'It's going to be brilliant!'

'I can't do it,' I said. 'Ciara's got her harvest festival.'

'Please tell me I'm not phoning these people up to say that you can't do it because you're going to Ciara's harvest festival!'

'Yeah, you'll have to,' I said. But in reality we've all missed things. Sometimes you just have to. And the kids are fine with it, as long as you get to the odd thing every now and then. You shouldn't feel guilty.   *Coleen*

I'll never forget Ben's first day at nursery. It was horrific. He only went for an hour, and I sat outside and cried harder than he did, I think. It sounds so silly, but it was one of the most difficult things I've ever done, because it was the first time I had to let go.   *Kate*

My family always come first, no matter what. If I was on *Loose Women* tomorrow and I got a call to say, 'One of the kids is sick, you need to come,' I would go immediately. If my boss said, 'You can't go. We'll fire you if you do,' I'd say, 'Well, fire me. I'm going home.'   *Coleen*

★ ★ ★

Staying at home

When I was married to Shane, I gave up work to be a stay-at-home mum for two and a half years. I absolutely loved it and didn't feel guilty at all, but it was probably the hardest two and a half years of my life! Being a housewife is a 24/7 job, with no thanks and no pay.

I also found that I became a bit invisible to other people. So if Shane got back from work and people came round to see us, they'd all be discussing what they'd been doing: 'How's your job going?' 'Great. How's yours?' No one would ever say to me, 'And how was your day?' because what could I say? 'Yeah, I washed the kitchen floor.' How exciting! Yet I really did enjoy that time.   *Coleen*

I was happy to be a housewife when I gave up work. I used to like doing the laundry; I used to change the beds, everything. I thought I was brilliant at it, but it's totally thankless and everybody thinks that you're being boring.   *Carol*

I read an article in the paper about two sisters: one is a stay-at-home domestic goddess and the other works 24/7 and is really stressed all the time. Their arguments are always about who is the most tired, who's doing the hardest job and who's the most stressed. My sister and I tend to have those types of arguments, because I work away from home and she doesn't have to, so I'm a bit envious of that. I get defensive if she criticises something that she thinks I'm not doing right. I say, 'Well, if you had to get up at four in the morning and go to London and work . . . !' But although she would admit that she is sometimes in the wrong, I also have to admit that I react so strongly because I'm guilty about being away from home and being so busy.   *Denise*

There's pressure on women to work and some women can't not work because that's what defines them. But I would have thought that if you were a mum and a homemaker, surely if you've created that kind of scenario, why wouldn't that define you? Why do you still have to go to work?   *Carol*

What is a Supermum? The media often like to use the label to describe a woman who 'does it all'; someone who goes back to a demanding job after having children. But some people might consider a Supermum to be someone who didn't go back to work, if they could afford not to. Or a mum in a low-income family struggling to bring up four or five children on her own. That's also being a Supermum in my book.   *Denise*

I work myself to death and am always aware that I've got to earn. I have a phobia about earning enough and looking after my daughter and my grandson in the future. My brother says, 'Sherrie, stop! As long as you can eat and pay your bills, and you're safe, and Keeley and Ollie are safe, that's all you need.' He's right, at the end of the day.   *Sherrie*

★ ★ ★

Me time

How do I pamper myself? Every Monday night I stay in London at a lovely hotel, after coming down to film *Loose Women*. That's pamper enough for me. I can lie on that bed after my shower and watch what I want and not move. Just that one night a week is like a little holiday, because I haven't got the kids and I'm not thinking that I'd better put the washing on or unload the dishwasher. Instead I've got room service! So I sit there like a slob. It's fantastic.   *Coleen*

'Go on, treat yourself Mum, have a sauna,'
her children said. But Sandra didn't
feel relaxed...she couldn't breathe!

Mums Were Kids Once, Too

Maybe your kids can't believe that you existed before they came along, but yes, you really did have a life BC (Before Children!). And that life was packed with all the antics and naughtiness that they're currently trying to get away with, not to mention a host of embarrassments, mistakes and aspirations. So don't let them think they can pull the wool over your eyes! Well, not much, anyway.

Every time I go to Blackpool, I drive by the little four-bedroom terrace on Waterloo Road where my family lived, all ten of us. I have such great memories of that house. I stop the car every time we go past and

Shane says, 'I know, Mum: there was only one bath-room; there were eight kids; I don't know how your mum did it; ooh, she used to have a mangle in the back garden!' He's heard it all so many times . . . *Coleen*

* * *

Childhood cringe

I was nine years old and playing Cinderella in a school production – my first lead role. The guy I had a crush on was playing Prince Charming and I was thrilled. The last scene was the happy-ever-after kiss. Of course, at nine, you're not going to do it in rehearsals. He was so embarrassed. 'We'll do it on the day,' we said.

I couldn't sleep for days beforehand, because I was so excited. The moment finally came: 'You'll live happily ever after . . .' I thought, *this is it!* I puck-ered up, but he just stood there, staring into the distance. He wouldn't kiss me! In the end, I had to lean forward and give him a kiss on the cheek. I cried for days! Humiliated at nine!   *Zoë*

In the three-legged race, I was always partnered with the one that couldn't do it. I'd end up dragging some-one up to the finishing line, moaning, 'Why do I always get the dope?' That made me lose my sense of compe-tition, because I felt I would never win.   *Sherrie*

I did a paper round from the age of ten. We had to get on a bus to go and get the papers, which was a pain when it was winter and really cold – I'm sure it was much colder in the Sixties than it is now. My grandma used to send us clothes and they were always really awful; we were never going to wear them. One day, a crocheted black and white tank top arrived. We looked at it and decided that there was no way we were wearing it, so my mum made it into a hat, in her enterprising way. It was horrible, but I had to wear it because it was really freezing and I had nothing else.

I was wearing it when I got on the bus to get my papers one day. The bus was a double-decker and it was full of people going to work. As I got off, the paper bag I was carrying was so heavy that it pulled me down and I fell forward and my tooth hit the kerb. But never mind my tooth and the grazed chin; all I could think was, the people on the bus are laughing at me because I'm wearing the hat! That moment has never left me.   *Carol*

I was four and I was on stage, about to sing, 'You've Gotta Have Heart'. I had to take my hat off, dress off, and I had a little tap outfit on underneath. You know when your mum says, 'Have you been?' Well, I hadn't. I got on stage and saw these people looking at me. I took my hat off and weed all over the floor. I never, ever got over it! I had to tap in all the wee.   *Sherrie*

* * *

Scary mums

My mum was very much from the school of tough
love. When I got grounded, I got properly grounded.
Once, I ran away to London and, quite rightly, she
kept me in for more than three months afterwards,
even though I pretended to go mad and went on
hunger strike. I was a delightful teenager!   *Kate*

I was scared of my mum, not because of what she would
do, but because I was really afraid of disappointing her.
I never once played truant; I never skived off school, not
for one single day, because I couldn't bear the thought
of my mum finding out. There were loads of things I did
that I made sure she never found out about. For instance,
I've got a little tattoo on my wrist, which I did myself
with a compass and some Indian ink. As soon as I'd done
it, I thought, 'Oh my God, what am I going to do? My
mum . . . !' So I went out and bought a big waterproof
Swatch watch to cover it. That watch was stuck to my

wrist; it never, ever came off. And my mum didn't actually find out about the tattoo until I was forty-three!   *Carol*

My mum always made a lovely blancmange. Once, I remember going on and on about wanting some of her blancmange. She must have been a bit premenstrual, because she literally dragged me to the fridge, said, 'You want the blancmange?' and shoved my head in a bowl of it!   *Kate*

My mum's mum was very strict. Once Mum got a letter at school and opened it. It said: 'We are very disappointed that Anne has been found smoking at school.' Instead of just not taking it home, my mother put in an arrow and changed it so that it read: 'We are very disappointed that Anne has ^ **not** been found smoking at school.' Then she sealed the envelope and took it home. Very clever!!!   *Denise*

I never talked to my mum as a friend or a mate or anything. I would have thought that was

a little bit weird. She was my mum. She gave
us discipline and a loving home.   *Carol*

Every time they caught me looking at myself in the mirror,
my parents would say, 'Stop smelling yourself!'   *Coleen*

* * *

'Elf and safety gone mad

Parents have been scared into not allowing their children to
take any risks. The Health and Safety Executive, for instance,
try to eliminate all risk and prevent all accidents, and you
can't do that. Kids learn from their mistakes. If you take
chances when you're young, you learn when to be more careful in life. My childhood was a health and safety nightmare!
The number of things we used to do that were unbeliev-
ably dangerous, like swing across rivers on ropes in the park.
They've probably fenced the entire river off now, so kids
can't do it, which I think is completely wrong.   *Carol*

If we no longer have kids climbing trees or jumping in ponds and the rest of it, the logical conclusion will be a world where we all have Botox, so we'll look like characters from the film *Avatar*; we'll be on walkways holding on to bars and everyone will speak very slowly. We'll all be very careful and very boring and it will be such a relief to die! Honestly, it's crazy. Get out there, kids, and enjoy your lives!   *Lynda*

★ ★ ★

Smokescreen

I started smoking when I was ten or eleven, because that's what everybody did. I knew I wasn't allowed to do it, because I was a child, but my mum did it and my sister was doing it. My first cigarette was revolting, but I was determined to like it, so I kept forcing myself. There was no awareness then of the health problems caused by smoking. There were no health warnings on the packets.

Everybody thought that this was what you did when you grew up: you started smoking. But now, I think it is so stigmatised and so socially unacceptable that it has been demonised to the point that kids want to do it. It's so naughty and wrong that it's almost illegal, almost less acceptable than drugs. Kids always want to do whatever is rebellious, so I think it's gone the other way now. *Carol*

I was well educated about the dangers of smoking. When I was at school, there was that ad campaign featuring Nick O'Teen, a sinister character who encouraged smoking. My dad has never smoked a cigarette in his life, but my mum was a smoker and when I was growing up, there were always cigarettes in the house. So I became a smoker. My mum has now, fabulously, given up, after years and years of twenty a day, but she only gave up because I gave up. She thought, 'If you can do it, I can do it.' She also did it for Ben, because she knew I didn't want her smoking around him. When I got pregnant, she said, 'Right, I'm going to do it.' I love her dearly for it. *Kate*

★ ★ ★

Childhood dreams

When I was eleven, I wanted to be a vet. Then I realised what qualifications you needed. I couldn't even spell degree, let alone get one. So I never got to fulfil my dream. (Sob!) Well, I kind of did, because I love dogs and now I'm working with them! You know I'm joking, don't you?   *Coleen*

Between eight and twelve, I wanted to be a fireman. Then I wanted to be a nun, after seeing *The Sound of Music*. I thought it looked fab: there's travel, romance, guitar playing! Next, I really wanted to be a journalist, so I went and did work experience on the local paper, but deep down, there was a quiet little kernel of a dream to be an actress. I was too shy though! I was brought up by beautiful, lovely but quite strict parents and acting was a wee bit like showing off. But in a way I have fulfilled my dream, as a presenter, because I pretend to be someone who knows what they're doing for an hour a day on *Loose Women*!   *Andrea*

★ ★ ★

Attention, please!

I was brought up by my mum, nan and granddad and I think they overcompensated for the fact that my mum and dad weren't together when I was born. They gave me tons of attention and I was absolutely ruined; I had pretty much everything. It was good in one sense, because I had really high self-esteem. I was really confident, which is good for kids. On the other hand, it was a responsibility, because if you feel that the attention is given to you because they don't want you to feel that something is missing in your life, it can put the pressure on. So it can work both ways. *Lisa*

* * *

Cooking lessons

My mum worked, so she wasn't interested in cooking, and because my nan was an old lady, she only made things like toad-in-the-hole, shepherd's pie, sausage and chips and egg and chips. Food was not a big thing for us. It was just to feed you. So I never had any interest in cooking and whenever I did try, my nan would say, 'Give it here! You're making a big mess out of it.' As a result, I never learnt to cook and I'm very embarrassed about it!   *Lisa*

I can cook anything. I learnt at school, where we did what we called DS, Domestic Science. I've still got my folder, which teaches you absolutely everything about cooking. I also learnt from watching my mum, who cooked fresh food every single day. OK, it was always potatoes. And she never washed the chip pan. She'd melt the lard, cook the chips, serve them out and put the pan back on the cooker. The lard would go hard again and it would just sit there until it was used again! You know what, though? They were great chips!   *Carol*

* * *

Cultural life

My parents aren't culture vultures. We didn't go to art galleries or anything, but they thought they were really highbrow by playing *Hooked on Classics*. The shock I had on learning that classical music didn't come with a disco beat in really short bursts! *Andrea*

★ ★ ★

Who's the favourite?

I was the baby of eight children. I was a little bit overlooked by my parents, because they didn't have time, but on the other hand I knew how to play it. If my brothers and sisters wound me up, I'd say, 'Mu-um!' All you'd hear from the kitchen was, 'Leave my baby alone!' They'd all go, 'Aw,' and I'd go, 'Yes!' So I did play on it a bit. But I still never felt that one sibling was favoured over the others in my family. *Coleen*

Scarlet was horrified but her Mum couldn't control herself. She hadn't been this excited since the Bay City Rollers came in to town!

Being a middle child can be difficult. I remember thinking about it quite often. There are four of us: there was my sister, who was the eldest; my brother, who was the only boy; and my other sister, who was the youngest. I was just in the middle, with no special status at all. I didn't feel unloved, but I was just No. 2. We always felt that my brother was the favourite, not because my mum loved him more, but because he was the boy. You know what mothers and sons are like. It wasn't that she spoiled him or preferred him, but there was a difference. Because we were quite poor, the eldest three had to get Saturday jobs and paper rounds to pay for things like our school uniform. By the time it came to my younger sister, I think my mum delighted in allowing her not to work, because that's what she would have liked to have done with all of us. But it meant we were always saying, 'How come she doesn't have to do a paper round?' *Carol*

* * *

No rowing rule

I came from a big family, so someone was always rowing, either the kids or Mum and Dad. My parents didn't argue all the time, but they did have rows. I'm completely the opposite. I can't bear shouting or rowing and I'm very non-confrontational.   *Coleen*

* * *

Tell on you!

I was certainly not the sensible sister. It was always me that was getting in trouble and Debbie was always 'telling'. She'd say, 'I'm telling, I'm telling!' At my first party I kissed Tommy Henderson. She interrupted our snog to say, 'I'm phoning Mum and Dad to tell!'   *Denise*

My sister had nothing to tell, because I was really dull! That meant that when my marriage ended and my life fell apart, it was really hard to cope with, because I'd always been 'the good girl'. I didn't know how to cope with it. My parents didn't know how to cope with it. We all ran around with our arms in the air for a while!   *Andrea*

★ ★ ★

Age of austerity

I think you have more respect for money if you grow up not having any, because you value it. I don't worship it – it's not the most important thing to me – but I don't waste it. I don't live beyond my means and I don't borrow money that I can't afford to pay back. I think that comes from growing up in a household where we went without. If we wanted to go swimming, we couldn't, because there was no money. So as soon as we all could, we went to work. I did a paper round at the age of eleven and I was paid 18 shillings a week, which is 90p, to get up every morning at 6 am, go to the paper shop on a bus, get the papers, walk back, do the paper round, which was about two or three miles, and go home. When you get 90p a week, you know where every penny of that money goes, and so I still know where every penny of my money goes.   *Carol*

* * *

Dirty tricks

When I was little, I got lost at Edinburgh Castle. We'd all been for a family day out; looking back at photos I see that I was wearing a little kilt and a little Aran jumper. I was wandering round the gift shop when I looked round to find my mum and dad had gone. They were hiding around the corner, just to see how long it would take me to realise. That was one of my earliest memories, of being abandoned by my parents!   *Andrea*

I love doing that with the kids! It's so funny to watch that moment of panic. Unfortunately, they always find me ... *Coleen*

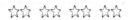

No seconds, please!

I was really thin as a child; I hated the food that my mum cooked for my dad, like belly pork and lamb shank with loads of fat on it. I used to gag on it! *Jane*

The things I ate when I was growing up were very different from the food I make for Finlay and Amy. My main memories of childhood food are of spam fritters and chips with a fried egg on top. I don't like that sort of thing now. *Andrea*

* * *

Boozy memories

Booze played a big part when I was growing up, because my parents had me when they were very young, when they were twenty-one. All the parties happened at our flat, so they could continue their social life without having to leave us. I remember going downstairs at four in the morning during the school holidays and saying, 'When are you all going home?' My parents and their friends would be dancing and drinking away! 'Oh, shut up!' they'd say. *Denise*

There wasn't much drinking in the house when I was young. We couldn't really afford booze; our treats were more about food. My mum worked in a pub, so if she wanted a drink, she could have one there. I think that's rubbed off on me a bit, because I don't drink much at home; I'd rather go to the pub. *Carol*

Being a binge-drinking teenager doesn't mean you'll be a boozer for life. I was a binger and my parents had to pick me up off the doorstep far too many times, but look at me now! (Three glasses of rosé and I'm on the floor next to Carol McGiffin!) *Kate*

Lovely Mums through the generations.

Acknowledgements

Following the success of our first four books *Girls' Night In*, *Here Come The Girls!*, *The Little Book of Loose Women* and *Loose Women On Men*, it has been a real pleasure to produce this book of our experiences and anecdotes on lovely mums. Once again a big thank you needs to go to our writer Rebecca Cripps for compiling our many stories and thoughts.

We would also like to thank the Loose Women production team who have worked on *The Loose Women Book for Lovely Mums*; in particular Fiona Keenaghan, Sharon Powers, Donna Gower, Kevin Morgan, Andy Whiting and Emily Humphries.

Last but not least, every good book needs a great publisher and we have been very lucky once again to have had the incredible support and talents of Hodder & Stoughton, in particular our editor Fenella Bates and her team Ciara Foley, Emma Knight, Kelly Edgson-Wright, Faith Booker and Susan Spratt.